Prepared in cooperation with the National Park Service

Ecological Thresholds as a Basis for Defining Management Triggers for National Park Service Vital Signs—Case Studies for Dryland Ecosystems

By Matthew A. Bowker, Mark E. Miller, R. Travis Belote, and Steven L. Garman

Open-File Report 2013–1244

U.S. Department of the Interior
U.S. Geological Survey

U.S. Department of the Interior
SALLY JEWELL, Secretary

U.S. Geological Survey
Suzette M. Kimball, Acting Director

U.S. Geological Survey, Reston, Virginia: 2013

For more information on the USGS—the Federal source for science about the Earth, its natural and living resources, natural hazards, and the environment, visit *http://www.usgs.gov* or call 1-888-ASK-USGS.

For an overview of USGS information products, including maps, imagery, and publications, visit *http://www.usgs.gov/pubprod*

To order this and other USGS information products, visit *http://store.usgs.gov*

Suggested citation:
Bowker, M.A., Miller, M.E., Belote, R.T., and Garman, S.L., 2013, Ecological thresholds as a basis for defining management triggers for National Park Service vital signs—Case studies for dryland ecosystems: U.S. Geological Survey Open-File Report 2013–1244, 94 p., http://pubs.usgs.gov/of/2013/1244/.

Contents

Introduction 1

    Background: Threshold and State-and-Transition Concepts 2

Methods Overview 4

    A General Approach to Applying Threshold Theory to Management 4

    Case Studies 5

    Northern Colorado Plateau Network (NCPN) Integrated Dataset 5

    Southern Colorado Plateau Network (SCPN) Data Sources 6

    Cluster Analyses 6

    Path Model-Based Simulation and Estimation of Thresholds 7

        A Priori Path Model 7

        Parameterization of Model and Simulation of Data 7

        Other Statistical Analyses 8

        Expert Opinion Surveys 8

Case Study 1: Semidesert Sandy Loam (Four Wing Saltbush) 9

    Background 9

    Method Details 9

        A Priori State-and-Ttransition Models 9

        Data 10

        Cluster Analyses 10

        Modeling Transitions 10

    Results 11

        Cluster Analysis: Semidesert Sandy Loam 11

        Final State-and-Transition Model 12

        Transitions and Threshold Estimation 14

    Interpretation 16

Case Study 2: Mesa Top Pinyon-Juniper 18

    Background 18

    Method Details 18

        A Priori State-and-Transition Models 18

    Data 19

        Cluster Analyses 19

        Temporal Dynamics 20

        Modeling Transitions 20

    Results 20

        Cluster Analysis 20

        Temporal Analysis 22

        Final State-and-Transition Model 23

        Transitions and Threshold Estimation 28

    Interpretation 31

Case Studies 3 and 4: Desert Shallow Sandy Loam (blackbrush) and Semidesert Shallow Sandy Loam (Utah juniper and pinyon pine) 33

    Background 33

    Method Details 33

        A Priori State-and-Transition Models 33

Data 34
   Cluster Analyses 34
Modeling Transitions 35
Results 36
   Cluster Analysis: Semidesert Shallow Sandy Loam 36
   Final State-and-Transition Model: Semidesert Shallow Sandy Loam 38
   Cluster Analysis: Desert Shallow Sandy Loam 40
   Final State-and-Transition Model: Desert Shallow Sandy Loam 41
   Transitions and Threshold Estimation 43
Interpretation 47
   Climate Change-Driven Transitions 48
Case Study 5: Semidesert Stony Loam (shadscale) 49
  Introduction 49
  Methods Details 49
   A Priori Model of Ecosystem Dynamics 49
   Data 50
   Cluster Analysis 50
   Modeling Transitions 50
  Results 51
   Cluster Analysis 51
   Final State-and-Transition Model 52
     Transitions and Threshold Estimation 54
  Interpretation 56
   Caveats and Alternative Explanations 57
Case Study 6: Clayey Fans 58
  Background 58
  Methods Details 58
   A Priori State and Transition Models 58
   Data 58
   Analysis of Grazing Impacts and Rebound from Grazing 59
   Cluster Analysis 60
   Modeling Transitions 60
  Results 60
   Temporal Transect Data 60
   Vegetation Map Data 62
   Grazing Dynamics 64
   Cluster Analysis 64
   Final State-and-Transition Model 66
     Catalog of States and Phases 67
   Transitions and Threshold Estimation 69
   Interpretation 70
Case Study 7: Limy Uplands 71
  Background 71
  Methods 71
   A Priori State-and-Transition Model 71
  Data 71
   Expert Opinion Surveys 72

Results.. 72
    Final State and Transition Model... 72
    Catalog of States and Phases—Final STM 73
    Confidence—Final STM 76
    Transitions and Threshold Estimation 76
Interpretation.. 78
Discussion.. 78
    Applying Threshold Concepts to Monitoring 81
Acknowledgments.. 82
References 82
Appendix 1: Expert Opinion Surveys 89
Appendix 2: Assessment and Tipping Points Quick Reference 93

Figures

Figure 1. Ordination of plots based on the four classification variables used in the fuzzy cluster analysis 12
Figure 2. State-and-transition diagram for Semidesert sandy loam 13
Figure 3. Path model articulating a predictive framework integrating both linear regressions and logistic regressions to result in a state transition probability output... 15
Figure 4. Path analysis-assisted multiple logistic regression models of the probability of transition from state 2 (to 3, given the values of three variables (aggregate stability, surface roughness, magnetic susceptibility) which are linked by the common causal influence of biological soil crusts... 16
Figure 5. Six versions of an NMDS ordination based on the 8 cluster solution 21
Figure 6. State-and-transition diagram for Pinyon-juniper Mesa Tops 26
Figure 7. Path model articulating a predictive framework integrating both linear regressions and logistic regressions to result in a state transition probability output... 29
Figure 8. Path model articulating a predictive framework integrating both linear regressions and logistic regressions to result in a state transition probability output... 30
Figure 9. Critical probabilities of transition from open woodlands to savannas as determined by two key drivers....... 31
Figure 10. NMDS ordination of a 5 cluster solution in 3 dimensions 36
Figure 11. Six versions of the above NMDS ordination, illustrating indicator species of the various clusters 37
Figure 12. State-and-transition diagram for semidesert shallow sandy loam. 38
Figure 13. NMDS ordination of a 3 cluster solution. 40
Figure 14. Three versions of the above NMDS ordination, illustrating indicator species of the 3 clusters. In each panel, the symbols are resized based on the abundance of a single species or biotic component. 41
Figure 15. State-and-transition diagram for desert shallow sandy loam... 41
Figure 16. A path model illustrating the hypothesized mechanism underlying T9 44
Figure 17. Modeled probabilities of transition from S1P4 to S2, given a range of grazing scenarios..................... 45
Figure 18. Linear regressions of soil stability as a function of biological soil crust cover. 46
Figure 19. State and transition model linking states and phases in Semidesert shallow sandy loam, and Desert shallow sandy loam due to drought-linked transitions.. 48
Figure 20. Image of the same ordination as above, with symbols resized to reflect the relative abundance of key species 51
Figure 21. State-and-transition diagram for Semidesert stony loam (shadscale). Solid boxes refer to ecosystem states, and dashed boxes represent phases within those states (red being at-risk of state transition)........................ 53
Figure 22. Logistic equations of Transitions 1,3, and 5, predicting the probability of transition................. 55

Figure 23. Increase in vegetation over time after the cessation of grazing on two transects on Clayey Fans............. 61
Figure 24. Vegetation change along Johnson (unpublished) transects.. 62
Figure 25. Vegetational differences among north (fenced later) and south (fenced earlier) clusters of Clayey Fans sampling sites 63
Figure 26. NMDS ordination of a 7 cluster solution in the first 2 of 3 dimensions. 65
Figure 27. Four versions of the above NMDS ordination, illustrating some of the indicator species of the various clusters 66
Figure 28. State and Transition Diagram for Clayey Fans 67
Figure 29. Modeled probabilities of transition from S1P4 to S4, given a range of total plant cover........................... 70
Figure 30. A state-and-transition model for Limy Uplands of Wupatki and surrounding areas................................. 73
Figure 31. Photographs showing (left panel) an extreme version of S1P3 (denuded grasslands) in 1907 and (right panel) S2 (savannized) in 1961 74

Tables

Table 1. Catalog of states and phases in Semidesert Sandy Loam. 14
Table 2. Cluster membership of samples through time 23
Table 3. Biological soil crust cover at critical points in the degradation of soil stability. 46
Table 4. Critical probabilities of transition given values of monitorable predictors for five transitions. 56
Table 5. Threshold estimates for five indicators of the transition from reference states to savannized states............. 77

Conversion Factors and Datum

Conversion factors

Multiply	By	To obtain
Length		
centimeter (cm)	0.3937	inch (in.)
meter (m)	3.281	foot (ft)
kilometer (km)	0.6214	mile (mi)
kilometer (km)	0.5400	mile, nautical (nmi)
meter (m)	1.094	yard (yd)
Area		
square hectometer (hm^2)	2.471	acre
square kilometer (km^2)	247.1	acre

Datum

Vertical coordinate information is referenced to North American Vertical Datum of 1988 (NAVD 88).
Elevation, as used in this report, refers to distance above the vertical datum.

Ecological Thresholds as a Basis for Defining Management Triggers for National Park Service Vital Signs—Case Studies for Dryland Ecosystems

By Matthew A. Bowker, Mark E. Miller, R. Travis Belote, and Steven L. Garman

Introduction

Threshold concepts are used in research and management of ecological systems to describe and interpret abrupt and persistent reorganization of ecosystem properties (Walker and Meyers, 2004; Groffman and others, 2006). Abrupt change, referred to as a threshold crossing, and the progression of reorganization can be triggered by one or more interactive disturbances such as land-use activities and climatic events (Paine and others, 1998). Threshold crossings occur when feedback mechanisms that typically absorb forces of change are replaced with those that promote development of alternative equilibria or states (Suding and others, 2004; Walker and Meyers, 2004; Briske and others, 2008). The alternative states that emerge from a threshold crossing vary and often exhibit reduced ecological integrity and value in terms of management goals relative to the original or reference system. Alternative stable states with some limited residual properties of the original system may develop along the progression after a crossing; an eventual outcome may be the complete loss of pre-threshold properties of the original ecosystem. Reverting to the more desirable reference state through ecological restoration becomes increasingly difficult and expensive along the progression gradient and may eventually become impossible. Ecological threshold concepts have been applied as a heuristic framework and to aid in the management of rangelands (Bestelmeyer, 2006; Briske and others, 2006, 2008), aquatic (Scheffer and others, 1993; Rapport and Whitford 1999), riparian (Stringham and others, 2001; Scott and others, 2005), and forested ecosystems (Allen and others, 2002; Digiovinazzo and others, 2010). These concepts are also topical in ecological restoration (Hobbs and Norton 1996; Whisenant 1999; Suding and others, 2004; King and Hobbs, 2006) and ecosystem sustainability (Herrick, 2000; Chapin and others, 1996; Davenport and others, 1998).

Achieving conservation management goals requires the protection of resources within the range of desired conditions (Cook and others, 2010). The goal of conservation management for natural resources in the U.S. National Park System is to maintain native species and habitat unimpaired for the enjoyment of future generations. Achieving this goal requires, in part, early detection of system change and timely implementation of remediation. The recent National Park Service Inventory and Monitoring program (NPS I&M) was established to provide early warning of declining ecosystem conditions relative to a desired native or reference system (Fancy and others, 2009). To be an effective tool for resource protection, monitoring must be designed to alert managers of impending thresholds so that preventive actions can be taken. This requires an understanding of the ecosystem attributes and processes associated with threshold-type behavior; how these attributes and processes become degraded; and how risks of degradation vary among ecosystems and in relation to environmental factors such as soil properties, climatic conditions, and exposure to stressors. In general, the utility of the threshold concept for long-term monitoring depends on the ability of scientists and managers to detect, predict,

1

and prevent the occurrence of threshold crossings associated with persistent, undesirable shifts among ecosystem states (Briske and others, 2006). Because of the scientific challenges associated with understanding these factors, the application of threshold concepts to monitoring designs has been very limited to date (Groffman and others, 2006). As a case in point, the monitoring efforts across the 32 NPS I&M networks were largely designed with the knowledge that they would not be used to their full potential until the development of a systematic method for understanding threshold dynamics and methods for estimating key attributes of threshold crossings.

This report describes and demonstrates a generalized approach that we implemented to formalize understanding and estimating of threshold dynamics for terrestrial dryland ecosystems in national parks of the Colorado Plateau. We provide a structured approach to identify and describe degradation processes associated with threshold behavior and to estimate indicator levels that characterize the point at which a threshold crossing has occurred or is imminent (tipping points) or points where investigative or preventive management action should be triggered (assessment points). We illustrate this method for several case studies in national parks included in the Northern and Southern Colorado Plateau NPS I&M networks, where historical livestock grazing, climatic change, and invasive species are key agents of change. The approaches developed in these case studies are intended to enhance the design, effectiveness, and management-relevance of monitoring efforts in support of conservation management in dryland systems. They specifically enhance National Park Service (NPS) capacity for protecting park resources on the Colorado Plateau but have applicability to monitoring and conservation management of dryland ecosystems worldwide.

Background: Threshold and State-and-Transition Concepts

Salient features among frameworks of ecological thresholds include concepts of reference conditions, feedback dynamics, threshold triggers, properties of the progression after a threshold crossing, and changes in restoration potential along this progression. Native or reference conditions typically are the desired state for conservation management, and consist of community phases and transitions among phases due to natural disturbances and climate variability. Negative feedbacks of the reference system confer system resilience and maintain the community phases within a characteristic range of variability. For instance, a negative feedback that inhibits shrub dominance in some grasslands is the interaction between amount of grass cover and fire return interval. Given sufficient grass cover, wildland fire events are frequent and large enough to maintain grassland structure because of the selective elimination of fire-intolerant woody plants. Phases comprising the natural range of reference conditions differ in their vulnerability to a threshold crossing. Phases with degraded resilience are more vulnerable and may be described as "at risk" of a persistent transition to an alternative state (Briske and others, 2008). Identifying the patterns that increase vulnerability to change, and identifying the underlying reasons for these patterns, can define preventive management goals (Bestelmeyer, 2006).

Biotic and abiotic mechanisms may trigger threshold crossings (Beisner and others, 2003; Briske and others, 2006). Biotic mechanisms include altered biotic structure and interactions, such as plant-herbivore interactions. Abiotic mechanisms (for example, extreme soil erosion) motivate threshold crossings through the modification of inherent site characteristics. A single trigger may initiate a threshold crossing, or the temporal order or spatial convergence of multiple triggers may be critical. For example, drought or intensive livestock grazing alone may not trigger a state change, but the two factors in combination or in sequence may trigger such a change through adverse effects of one stressor on ecosystem resilience to the other stressor (Scheffer and others, 2001). Triggers result in conditions that exceed the resilience of the reference system and lead to an increasing dominance of positive, destabilizing feedbacks. Triggers often initiate changes in the pattern or spatial structure of an

2

ecosystem (for example, decreased vegetation cover or increased patchiness) with subsequent and often non-linear changes in processes (for example, soil erosion and nutrient cycling; Peters and others, 2004).

The progression after a threshold crossing is characterized by increasing dominance of positive feedbacks and changes in pattern and processes (Briske and others, 2008). As this progression unfolds, there is a continual loss of properties of the reference condition. Multiple alternative states, each with their own set of varying community phases, can occur along this threshold progression with some states becoming stable as negative feedbacks of the alternative state confers resilience. Progression can lead to a degraded state where features of the reference condition are effectively no longer present. Degraded states may no longer afford provision of services such as water, livestock forage production, or desirable recreational opportunities, and may no longer support the biodiversity of native systems.

The potential for restoration to pre-threshold conditions is determined by the amount of residual properties of the reference condition and the resilience of the new, alternative state (Suding and Hobbs, 2009). Where extensive site preparation and reintroduction of native species are required for conversion to pre-threshold conditions, the costs may effectively prohibit restoration. In some cases, complete restoration to native conditions may never be possible because of the extinction of native biota (that is, species and genomes) or the loss of inherent properties (for example, soil fertility) necessary to support reference conditions.

Focused study and interpretation of threshold processes and consequences benefit from using conceptual models of ecosystem dynamics. State-and-transition models (STMs) are a type of conceptual model that have become prominent in rangeland management and are used to illustrate reference conditions of an ecosystem, ecosystem responses to natural and anthropogenic drivers, and the mechanisms of transition among distinctive states of an ecosystem (Bestelmeyer and others, 2003, 2009). These models also provide a basis for discerning levels of system properties indicative of the risk and occurrence of transition among states (Briske and others, 2008).

Identifying indicator levels signaling an impending threshold crossing is a critical component in the design of effective monitoring. Monitoring efforts should result in alerting land managers of indicator levels in advance of a threshold crossing, to account for lag-time in decision making and uncertainty in the effectiveness of remediation actions. From a statistical perspective, the number and frequency of monitoring observations required to provide early warning is dependent on the differences among the current status of the indicator, the early-warning status level, and the inherent spatial and temporal variability of the indicator. Realistically, given uncertainty in early-warning levels and inherent variability of indicators, monitoring resources are likely insufficient to statistically detect a declining trend within a time period sufficient for decision making (Field and others, 2004). Bennetts and others (2007) have proposed the use of management assessment points along a continuum of indicator values to safeguard against uncertainties in estimates of threshold crossings, in indicator variability, and in the efficacy of a monitoring or sampling design. We propose that indicator values associated with key critical probabilities of transition are useful assessment points. However, a fundamental component for establishing assessment points are credible estimates of resource and environmental conditions indicative of impending threshold crossings. Here we provide a means of making reasonable estimates of indicators used in NPS I&M programs corresponding to probabilistic assessment points in several ecosystems.

Methods Overview

A General Approach to Applying Threshold Theory to Management

We developed a general approach for identifying properties of thresholds to inform estimates of management assessment points in a long-term monitoring context. Our approach relies on using conceptual models of threshold dynamics and various sources of information to verify the conceptual model, and to make informed estimates of threshold crossings and associated indicator values:

(1) Identification of target ecosystems.—We adopted the U.S. Department of Agriculture Natural Resource Conservation Service (USDA NRCS) ecological site concept as a framework for ecosystem classification and model development. Ecological sites are land units differentiated by (a) physical attributes including inherent soil properties (texture, depth, and horizonation), geomorphic setting, and climate; (b) the potential (rather than current) vegetation associated with these physical attributes within a specific ecoregion; and (c) characteristic dynamics in response to climate, management, and other driving factors (Herrick and others, 2005; Bestelmeyer and others, 2009).

(2) Conceptual models of system dynamics.—We developed STMs to organize current knowledge or hypotheses about the dynamics and community phases of specific ecological sites, the key alternative states representative of degradation pathways, and the transitions that are possible among these states. Possible triggers of transitions among alternative states and pattern and process indicators of specific degradation pathways were identified or hypothesized based on published literature, unpublished expert knowledge of an ecological site, or general ecological principles. Identifying triggers is most useful because observations of their occurrence could initiate preventative management actions. This process- and theory-based focus in the construction of the STM, contrasts with pattern-based efforts which seek to define states based on classification of multivariate community structure data (for example, Allen-Diaz and Bartolome, 1998). These data-driven approaches offer the credibility of being based on real data, but assume that a dataset is likely to capture all of the important states that are possible within a given ecological site, and that the identified states are fundamentally and functionally distinct (Bestelmeyer and others, 2003). We instead advocate using available data to test specific elements of *a priori* process-based conceptual STMs, as a means of calibrating and validating the model.

(3) Model calibration.—Model building is an iterative process, and it is important to include a calibration step. Calibration included testing the concepts presented in the model using available datasets, or subjecting them to the scrutiny of an expert panel. This enables an opportunity to revise the model; identify new transitions and associated triggers, processes and indicators; and allow an estimation of confidence that the revised model is reasonable.

(4) Identification of key transitions and estimation of tipping and assessment points.—The calibrated model is used to identify the most likely transitions that might be detected by a monitoring program, emphasizing those known to be of concern to management, such as the persistent conversion of perennial grasslands to ecosystems dominated by invasive annuals or woody plants. The values of key indicators at the point of a threshold crossing (when one state abruptly transitions to another) are estimated. We refer to these as tipping points; they are approximately equivalent to restoration thresholds (in the sense of Bestelmeyer, 2006). In the present work (2013), we typically apply a probabilistic definition to the tipping point concept—the point at which a transition is nearly certain, or 95 percent probable. Because abrupt transitions-in-progress are seldom observed, statistical methods are used to model the tipping points in indicator values using samples representative of discrete states. In data-sparse situations, these estimates are derived from expert knowledge rather than statistical modeling. The assessment points are another set of indicator values which trigger management action prior to observing a tipping point, so that the undesired transition can be avoided. These values occur chronologically before tipping points and allow managers sufficient response time. They are based on the range of natural variability in the reference or less-degraded state when data are available or based on the opinions from an expert panel when data are lacking. Again, in the present work we use a recurring set of critical transition probabilities as an operational definition of assessment points: 5 percent is the point at which a transition is reasonably possible, 25 percent is the point at which a transition ceases to be an uncommon event, and 50 percent is the point at which a transition or lack thereof are equally probable.

Case Studies

We present seven case studies that illustrate different methods for identifying assessment points based on contrasting scenarios of data availability and quality. The case studies represent ecological sites in NPS units on the Colorado Plateau, where the general monitoring goal is to provide early warning of system decline in sufficient time for management actions to avert impending undesirable changes. At one end of the gradient, there is a data-rich case study, Semidesert sandy loam (Fourwing saltbush [*Atriplex canescens*]), for which a single large, spatially replicated range assessment dataset was available. Using a single large dataset is preferable because it sidesteps the issue of observer and study bias. The Mesa Top Pinyon-Juniper ecosystem of Bandelier National Monument is another data rich case study in which a single dataset adds a rich temporal component. Other case studies represent situations for which data from multiple imperfect sources exist, including Semidesert shallow sandy loam (Blackbrush [*Coleogyne ramosissima*]-Utah juniper [*Juniperus osteosperma*]), Desert shallow sandy loam (Blackbrush), Mesa top pinyon [*Pinus edulis*]-juniper [*Juniperus monosperma*], and Semidesert stony loam (Shadscale [*Atriplex confertifolia*]). In these cases, data from various sources were pooled to increase replication, increase spatial coverage, or include important gradients and stressors. There also were several data-sparse ecological sites for which only some data existed. The data was either not comprehensive in terms of capturing community structure and ecosystem function, or poorly replicated in space or time. These sites included Clayey fans and Limy uplands. Methods for each case study are summarized briefly in the following paragraphs, and described more fully in the following sections devoted to case studies.

Northern Colorado Plateau Network (NCPN) Integrated Dataset

We compiled an integrated dataset from multiple sources with representation of several ecological sites found in the NPS I&M Northern Colorado Plateau network: Semidesert sandy loam (Fourwing saltbush), Desert shallow sandy loam (Blackbrush), Semidesert shallow sandy loam (Pinyon Pine-Utah Juniper-Blackbrush), Semidesert stony loam (Shadscale), among others. 627 cases (plot-level datapoints) were compiled from 7 data sources. These include: (1) the Arches National Park vegetation mapping dataset (Coles and others, 2009), which provides plant community composition and some ground cover data by cover class; (2) the Capitol Reef National Park vegetation mapping dataset (Clark and others, 2009), which provides quantitative plant community composition and some ground cover data from two data collection periods and multiple disturbance regimes; (3) the NPS I&M network dataset (Witwicki, 2009a, 2009b), which provides quantitative plant community composition, soil stability, gap size distributions, ground cover, and multiple years of sampling; (4) the Grand Staircase-Escalante National Monument rangeland health assessment data set (Miller, 2008), which provides quantitative plant community data, soil stability, and ground cover; (5) Bowker and others (in press), which provides plant community composition, soil stability, gap size distributions, ground cover among other data, and multiple disturbance histories in the Dugout Ranch and portions of Canyonlands; (6) the

Canyonlands vegetation mapping dataset (J. Belnap, US Geological Survey, written commun. 2011) and (7) the NPS monitoring protocol development dataset (Miller and others, 2007), which provides plant community composition, soil stability, gap size distributions, and ground cover among other data.

Time since grazing is estimated conservatively by subtracting the last possible date of grazing activity from the date of data collection. In the case of the NCPN dataset, the first year of plot establishment was used. In the entire database, this calculation resulted in time since grazing estimates of: 0, 3, 10, 14, 20, 21, 26, 27, 31, 32, 33, 34, and 44 years, and never grazed.

Southern Colorado Plateau Network (SCPN) Data Sources

Unlike in the NCPN, each unit in the SCPN tends to be highly individualistic with little overlap of ecological sites. In addition, there are fewer data resources in general, which makes it less useful to integrate multiple datasets to boost replication and capture important variation; instead, we analyzed the individual datasets deemed to be most useful. For the Mesa Top Pinyon-Juniper ecological site of Bandelier National Monument, we focused our efforts on a watershed-scale monitoring dataset that spanned 15 years and captured restoration manipulations and drought (Hastings and others, 2003). For the Clayey Fans ecological site of Petrified Forest National Park, we used a set of 128 plots with plant community composition and cover data that were initially part of the production of a vegetation map (Thomas and others, 2009). To capture response to grazing release, we also analyzed unpublished data reported by Johnson (G. Johnson, National Park Service, unpubl. data, 1984), and Rowlands (P. Rowlands, National Park Service, unpubl. data, 1992), derived from two transects monitored for 20 years.

Cluster Analyses

To validate the existence of the states proposed in *a priori* STMs, we used cluster analyses when sufficient data existed. We considered a cluster to be roughly equivalent to a state or phase. We used two different techniques among the various ecological sites depending on exactly what data we determined to cluster. Both techniques having strengths and weaknesses. Hierarchical cluster analyses were applied in cases where we analyzed a species abundance matrix, we used Ward's method with a flexible beta. Distance among samples was defined as Bray-Curtis distance. The compatibility with multiple distance measures provides a flexibility to hierarchical clustering; most community datasets are not distributed in such a way that Euclidean distance should be used. In one case where we analyzed a matrix containing plant functional groups and other functional properties of the site such as biological soil crust (may be abbreviated as biological crust or biocrust in figures due to space constraints) cover and bare ground cover, we used fuzzy cluster analysis (Equihua, 1990). Fuzzy clustering methods offer more flexibility than hierarchical clustering when attempting to group elements which may overlap or have vague boundaries, such as states. It calculates degree of cluster membership, and a sample may have some degree of affinity with multiple clusters. This method is compatible only with Euclidean distance; use of this distance measure is justified by approximate normal distributions of data, approximate linear intercorrelation among variables, and few zero values. In our analyses, we selected the number of clusters partially based on information remaining and partially based on our prior of how many clusters there may be (McCune and Grace, 2002). Hierarchical cluster analyses were conducted in PC-ORD™ 4.0 (MJM Software Design) and fuzzy cluster analyses were conducted in NCSS™ 2001 software (Hintze, 2004).

Path Model-Based Simulation and Estimation of Thresholds

A Priori Path Model

Each transition among states or phases is related to a set of interrelationships among system components. For example, consumption of herbaceous forage by grazing animals may decrease fire frequency which may enable tree colonization. This set of interactions might be expressed as a path diagram of the form: grazing→fire frequency→tree density. Such systems underlying transitions may be simple or complex and can be well-described by a path model. A path model is a construct for organizing known or hypothesized behaviors in systems and can be used (1) to test the probability that the model captures the correct causal structure, (2) to partition the multiple effects that one system component can have on another, and (3) to make a prediction. The path diagram serves as a visualization of the model. It illustrates relationships among variables in a network. Normally, a relationship among variables is described as a linear function. In our applications, the end point of the path models is state membership, a binary variable. It may have one or more direct predictors. These predictors may have causal interrelationships. Finally, the predictors may in turn be predicted by one or more upstream predictor variables that do not directly influence state membership. A causal relationship is indicated by a directed arrow. Using linear regressions we established the mathematical relationships expressed in the path model using available data. State membership was predicted as a multiple logistic function of multiple variables in the model. When considering membership in one state or the other, the output is the probability that a sample will belong to, for example "state 2" rather than "state 1". Although this predicts state membership in a static dataset in most cases, from a frequentist perspective, it might be considered the probability of transition from one state to another. This assumption is strengthened when data from before and after an apparent transition are available for the same set of samples.

Parameterization of Model and Simulation of Data

We separately parameterized each of these linear and logistic regression equations (see previous section) for each arrow in the model, estimating slopes and intercepts, and error about the regression line. This system of equations, solved in the "upstream" to "downstream" sequence, illustrated in the path model formed the basis of the simulation of data with the correlative structure of the real data. The advantage of simulated data is that we can produce a large sample size, and can interpolate holes in the sampling scheme. Each linear regression was modeled with an appropriate amount of random error (based on the root mean square error [RMSE], the standard deviation around the regression line). This was accomplished in a Microsoft® Excel spreadsheet wherein the linear regression formula referenced the x data in one column, and the output and estimate of y in another column. We simulated error following a normal distribution using the Microsoft® Excel function = Norms(Rand( ), μ, sd). Where Norms simulates a standard normal distribution, the Rand function generates random numbers, μ represents the mean value, which is approximated by the output of the corresponding regression equation. The sd represents the standard deviation of the distribution, and is approximated by the standard deviation of the data around the corresponding regression line. In order to simulate a wide variety of combinations of the predictors of probability of transition, we generally solved the system of equations, with error, for the entire range of plausible values for the farthest "upstream" variable. For example, if the farthest upstream variable was time since grazing, we might solve the system of equations for every 0.5 year from 0 to 50. We solved this 100 separate times, which enabled us to calculate a mean probability of transition and the 95-percent confidence interval for each value. We determined the values of all variables in the network at critical probabilities. Our critical probablitities were: 5 percent, the threshold beyond which transitions are a reasonable possibility; 95 percent, the threshold beyond which transitions are almost certain; 50 percent, the threshold at which transition or lack thereof are equiprobable; and 25 percent, the threshold beyond which transitions cease to be rare. The 95 percent value can be considered to be similar to a tipping point, whereas the other values might be viewed as assessment points.

Other Statistical Analyses

We often used non-metric multidimensional scaling (NMDS) ordinations or occasionally other ordination techniques as a visual tool to illustrate cluster analysis results. Correlations of individual species with ordination axes helped us to determine and illustrate how clusters differed from one another. Model simulations of some transitions did not warrant a complex treatment like the path model assisted simulations described above (preceding section). These transitions were simply modeled using either linear or logistic regression.

Expert Opinion Surveys

Because of the incomplete nature of the available data for data-sparse case studies, we pursued an alternative strategy for the validation of the states and dynamics delineated in the STM. Our approach has much in common with the Delphi technique of engaging expert opinion panels in that it is a multiphase, iterative approach, that uses a "straw-document" as a starting point and engages participants individually so that outputs are not disproportionately affected by dominant personalities (Linstone and Turoff, 1975; Oliver, 2002). This approach has proven to be useful when, "the problem does not lend itself to precise analytical techniques but can benefit from subjective judgements on a collective basis" (Linstone and Turoff, 1975, Page 4). We constructed email-based questionnaires in two stages: (1) model calibration and (2) estimation of tipping and assessment points in indicators that enable detection of proximity to threshold crossings. Based on literature findings, and past experience, we drafted a STM including a catalog of states, phases, and transitions. We identified a list of potential expert consultants and recruited them to participate in the survey. The format of the model calibration survey included a draft STM including a diagram and a description of state charcateristics, and a questionnaire asking respondents to identify any states, phases, or transitions that should be removed from or added to the model. Our questionnaires specifically use estimates of confidence in responses, an important measure of uncertainty. We revised the model, according to respondent comments. We also calculated an aggregate confidence value. The second phase of the survey was more focused on thresholds associated with key transitions. This survey consisted of a revised STM with aggregate confidence values and a questionnaire in which respondents were presented with a set of indicators and characteristic units and then asked to estimate tipping and assessment points for each. Responses were average-weighted by confidence to estimate tipping and assessment points.

Case Study 1: Semidesert Sandy Loam (Four Wing Saltbush)

Background

The Semidesert sandy loam (SDSL) ecological site is widely distributed throughout the Colorado Plateau region of North America and is significant for past and current use for livestock grazing (USDA NRCS major land resource area 35, ecological site 035XY215UT). This ecological site occurs on flat to gently sloping landforms at 1,310–2,010 m elevation and receives 20–30 cm mean annual precipitation. Soils are formed in moderately deep to very deep (from 50 to greater than 150 cm) aeolian and alluvial deposits from sandstone and are moderately alkaline with sandy loam or loamy sand texture. In relatively undisturbed settings, the vascular plant community typically has a grassland aspect and is characterized by a mixture of perennial C_3 (*Hesperostipa comata* and *Achnatherum hymenoides*) and C_4 (*Sporobolus* spp.) bunchgrasses, C_4 rhizomatous grasses (*Pleuraphis jamesii* and *Bouteloua gracilis*), shrubs, and annual herbaceous species. In contrast with many dryland ecosystems, most common shrubs (for example, *Krascheninnikovia lanata* and *Atriplex canescens*) are palatable to livestock and shrub-dominated communities can occur with long-term absence of livestock grazing. Plant nomenclature here and throughout follows Natural Resources Conservation Service (2010). Biological soil crust (Belnap, 2003) is another biotic functional type that is a characteristic component of relatively undisturbed SDSL sites (Kleiner and Harper, 1972; Bowker and Belnap, 2008). Biological soil crusts have yet to be widely incorporated in conceptualizations of dryland ecosystem dynamics despite evidence of their functional significance for soil stabilization (Belnap, 1995; Warren, 2003), nutrient cycling (Evans and Lange, 2003), hydrologic processes (Warren, 2003), and mediation of plant establishment (Belnap and others, 2003; Escudero and others, 2007). Biological soil crusts also are notable for their lack of resistance to surface disturbances which can result in long-term reductions in spatial continuity, biological diversity, physical structure, and functionality (Belnap and Eldridge, 2003; Miller, 2008).

Canyonlands National Park preserves regionally significant examples of SDSL ecosystems that remain relatively undisturbed by human activities exclusive of anthropogenic atmospheric changes. Within Canyonlands National Park, however, there also are extensive examples of SDSL ecosystems with persistently degraded composition, structure, and function attributable to impacts of past livestock grazing (for example, Neff and others, 2005; Belnap and others, 2009). Domestic livestock were introduced to this area in the late 1880s and portions of Canyonlands were grazed by livestock until 1974. Livestock grazing remains an important economic activity on adjacent lands outside Canyonlands. Unlike many semiarid grasslands, neither fire nor frequent grazing by herds of large mammals are characteristic natural disturbances associated with the SDSL site. Thus grazing and associated surface disturbances by livestock represent novel disturbances in this system.

Method Details

A Priori State-and-Transition Models

Field observations, published literature (Kleiner and Harper, 1972; Neff and others, 2005; Belnap and others, 2009), and an existing USDA NRCS ecological site description (USDA NRCS ecological site 035XY215UT) provided the basis for developing a STM articulating hypotheses about system dynamics, degradation pathways among alternative states, and associated ecosystem patterns, processes, and feedbacks. The conceptual model identifies four ecosystem states based on persistent differences in the relative abundance of biotic functional types. States one and two are dominated by biological soil crusts. State one lacks functionally significant invasive exotic annuals (for example,

Bromus tectorum or *Salsola* sp.), whereas they are present in state two. The first state represents the desired condition relative to NPS management goals, whereas states two through four represent increasing degrees of degradation to be avoided or mitigated. The third state is characterized by the replacement of biological soil crust by bare ground and a vascular plant community dominated by perennial grasses or palatable shrubs with significant levels of invasive annuals. The fourth state is characterized by persistent dominance by invasive annual grasses or forbs.

Data

The best available dataset is derived from a broad-scale ecosystem inventory project purposefully designed to characterize ranges of variability in key compositional and structural attributes of dryland ecosystems in Canyonlands National Park and on adjacent lands currently used for livestock grazing (Miller and others, 2011; Bowker and others, *in press*). These inventory data were collected over a 3-year period and do not quantify temporal transitions among states. However, through a combination of targeted sampling and extensive spatial replication (substituting space for time) with random sampling, this dataset documents current ranges of variability for the SDSL and provides a relatively rich basis for estimating tipping points and associated assessment points. The dataset quantified variability among 72 SDSL plots on a single soil type (Begay series; see Bowker and others, *in press* for information on additional soil types) on the basis of live cover of biological soil crusts (moss, lichen, cyanobacterial crust cover summed; excluding physical crusts primarily aggregated by physical or chemical mechanisms) and vascular plants, ground cover, and indicators of erosion resistance including soil aggregate stability, spacing between perennial plant canopies, and spacing between perennial plant bases (Miller and others, 2011; sampling methods followed from Herrick and others, 2005). Sampling was conducted both within and outside Canyonlands National Park to ensure that the dataset included a wide range of ecosystem conditions.

Cluster Analyses

To validate the existence of the states proposed in our *apriori* STM, fuzzy cluster analysis (Equihua, 1990) was applied to four state properties including biological soil crust cover, bare ground cover, combined cover of perennial grasses and palatable shrubs, and relative cover of invasive exotic annuals based on a Bray-Curtis distance matrix. Fuzzy clustering methods offer more flexibility than hierarchical clustering when attempting to group elements which may overlap or have vague boundaries, such as states.

Modeling Transitions

Based on available literature, we hypothesized that one of the transitions may be largely detected because of the abundance of biological soil crust but is functionally related to the loss of soil aggregating and resource capturing activities attributable to the biological soil crust. Biological soil crusts are well-documented to provide a large degree of soil aggregate stabilization in otherwise poorly aggregated sandy soils, decreasing erodibility and the potential for erosion (Bowker and others, 2008; Chaudhary and others, 2009; Belnap and others, 2009). They maintain surface roughness, by preserving the uplift created by winter frost heaving. Surface roughness may influence capture of resources such as water by reducing the energy of overland flow, and increasing the probability of infiltration (Belnap and others, 2003). Both surface roughness and aggregate stability promote retention of exogenous dust-borne nutrients (Reynolds and others, 2001). Roughness enhances initial dust capture because low lying points on a roughened surface naturally function as dust sinks, and high points provide shelter from erosive forces. Soil aggregation and production of sticky polysaccharides enhance the proportion that is retained. Because local sandstone parent materials are poor in magnetic materials, and exogenous wind transported material is comparatively magnetic, magnetic susceptibility has been used as an index of entrained dust within local areas. Some of these relationships are truly feedbacks; for example, it is thought that early in biological soil crust succession, greater surface roughness will promote biological soil crust colonization rates (Davidson and others, 2002). However, this relationship quickly switches and roughness becomes an outcome of biological soil crust growth, age, and development. Thus, generally speaking, many of these assymetrical feedbacks can be approximated with simple linear one way relationships.

Using linear regressions, we estimated the slopes and intercepts of the estimated linear relationships among biological soil crust cover and biological soil crust functional indicators. For example, aggregate stability can be modeled as a linear function of biological soil crust cover, and the slope and intercept terms can be estimated from available data. Appropriate transformations were applied to biological soil crust cover data and soil aggregate stability data to improve linearity (Bowker and others, 2008). We also conducted a multiple logistic regression with the predictors surface roughness, aggregate stability, and magnetic susceptibility upon the binary response of state membership. Multicollinearity can cause errors in the estimation of individual slopes of correlated predictors, however it does not affect the overall model performance. Thus is in a predictive context such as this, it does not constitute a problem.

In order to use these equations in a predictive framework with a realistic degree of stochasticity, we input all these relationships into a spreadsheet. Roughness and aggregate stability were predicted outcomes. Biological soil crust cover was assumed to be known without error, but the values of roughness, aggregate stability and magnetic susceptibility were random draws from the expected normal distributions. These estimates, of reasonable roughness, aggregate stability, and magnetic susceptibility values based on a given level of biological soil crust cover, were then input into the multiple logistic regression equation described in the preceding paragraph to generate a probability of membership in one of two ecosystem states. Under a space-for-time replacement scenario, this probability might be considered equivalent to the probability of transition occurring.

Using this simulation framework we solved the system of equations for all possible values of biological soil crust cover, the ultimate causal agent in the model, in 0.5 percent increments from 0 to 100 percent. We repeated the simulation 100 times, averaging the probabilities of transition and computing their standard deviations.

Exploratory analyses indicated that the transition from S3 to S4 was less suited to this path model assisted technique because upstream relationships were not particularly strong and had poor predictive power. Instead, we applied a simple logistic regression approach of cluster membership as a function of relative exotic cover.

Results

Cluster Analysis: Semidesert Sandy Loam

The cluster analysis distinguished three clusters analogous to states in our *a priori* conceptual model, and provided no evidence for states not included in the model (fig. 1). Our *a priori* model hypothesized a reference state lacking invasive plants entirely and supporting biological soil crusts. The reason this state was not detected is that all sites contained invasive annual grasses to some degree. Thus, a biological soil crusted state with a mild degree of invasion may be the current potential for this ecological site.

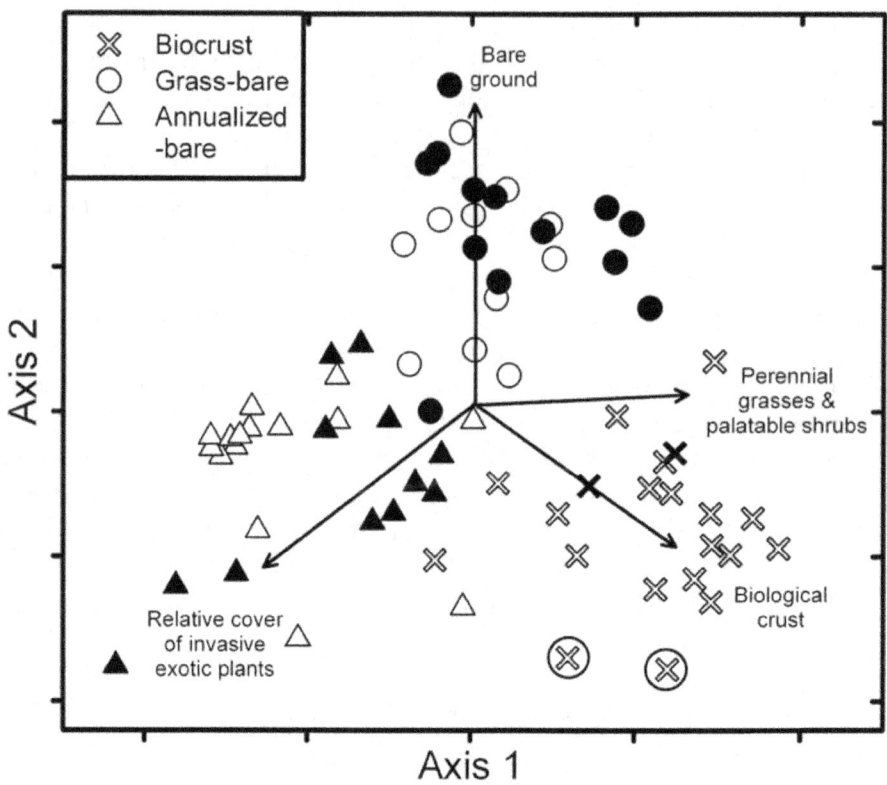

Figure 1. Ordination of plots based on the four classification variables used in the fuzzy cluster analysis. Clusters are noted as *Biocrust*, *Grass-bare*, and *Annualized-bare*. Closed symbols indicate plots that are currently accessible to grazing, open symbols indicate plots that formerly were grazed, and circled open symbols indicate two plots that were never grazed. Vectors indicate loadings of four classification variables on the two axes.

Final State-and-Transition Model

Our final state and transition model (fig. 2) synthesizes the results of the cluster analysis with observed heterogeneity on the landscape. The model suggests palatable shrub and perennial grass dominated phases of each of the first three states. These phases freely intergrade and create a fine scale mosaic. S4, the annualized state also has two phases: one dominated by *B. tectorum* and one by *Salsola* spp. These also intergrade. It is common to find both co-occurring, although dominance tends to shift from *B. tectorum* to *Salsola* as elevation or precipitation decrease. We describe the states and phases in table 1.

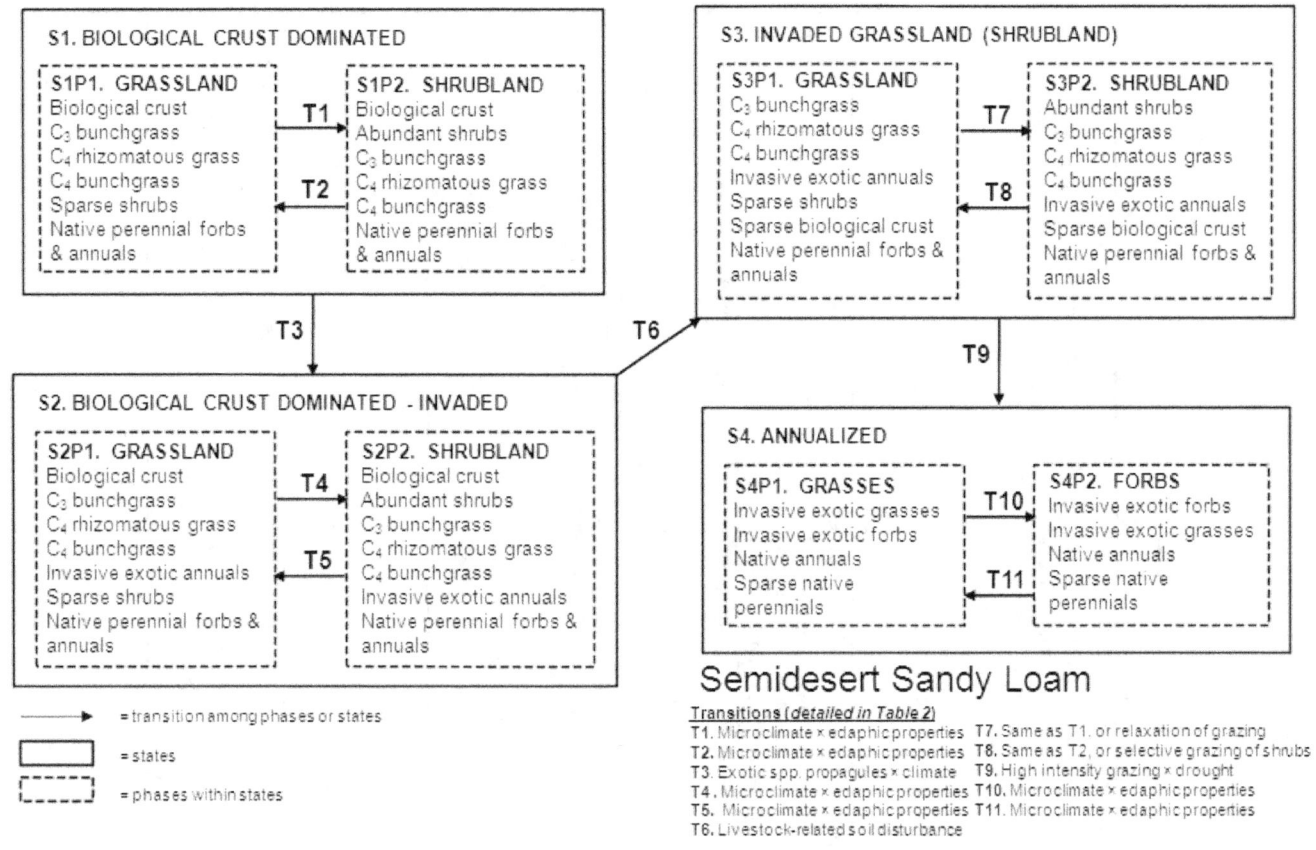

Figure 2. State-and-transition diagram for Semidesert sandy loam. Solid boxes refer to ecosystem states and dashed boxes represent phases within those states.

Table 1. Catalog of states and phases in Semidesert sandy loam.

State	Phase	Structural properties	Functional properties	Feedbacks
S1. Biological soil crust dominated	P1. Grassland	Biological soil crust dominant or co-dominant relative to vascular plants; perennial grasses abundant relative to shrubs, with variable grass composition due to climate fluctuations, soil variability, site history. High degree of soil-surface roughness.	High biological soil crust cover maintains high capacity for resource capture and retention (including nutrients, water, litter, seeds) even with flucations in plant cover. [1,2]	High resource retention promotes plant community resilience to climatic fluctuations and natural disturbance.
	P2. Shrubland	Similar to S1P1 but with palatable shrubs abundant relative to perennial grasses.	Same as S1P1.	Same as S1P1.
S2. Biological soil crust dominated -- invaded	P1. Grassland	Similar to S1P1 but invasive exotic annuals present. Cover of invasive annuals fluctuates with climate.	Similar to S1P1, but presence of invasive annuals can cause greater climate-driven fluctuations in cover and production relative to S1P1.	Same as S1P1.
	P2. Shrubland	Similar to S1P2 but invasive exotic annuals present. Cover of invasive annuals fluctuates with climate.	Similar to S1P2, but presence of invasive annuals can cause greater climate-driven fluctuations in cover and production relative to S1P2.	Same as S1P2.
S3. Invaded grassland (or shrubland)	P1. Grassland	Biological soil crust replaced by bare ground; otherwise similar to S2P1. Major decline in soil-surface roughness relative to S1P1 and S2P1.	Loss of stability and roughness associated with biological soil crust result in major decline in site capacity for resource capture and retention; accelerated losses of soil, nutrients, water, litter, and seeds occur. [1,2]	Accelerated losses of soil resources and seeds contribute to declines in plant community resilience to climatic fluctuations and to declines in vegetative cover and production, which result in further declines in site resistance to erosion and resource loss.
	P2. Shrubland	Biological soil crust replaced by bare ground; otherwise similar to S2P2. Major decline in soil-surface roughness relative to S1P2 and S2P2.	Similar to S3P1, although rates of resource loss may be greater in shrubland due to relative lack of perennial grass cover.	Same as S3P1.
S4. Annualized	P1. Grasses	Dominated by invasive exotic annual grasses (for example, *Bromus*). Native annuals may present but perennials sparse.	Dominance by annuals results in high fluctuations in cover due to climate with corresponding high (and potentially extreme) fluctuations in resource loss/erosion [2].	Same as S3P1, but greater. Potential spiraling declines in resource availability and site productivity. [1]
	P2. Forbs	Dominated by invasive exotic annual forbs (for example, *Salsola*). Native annuals may be present, but perennials sparse.	Same as S4P1.	Same as S4P1.

14

[1] Neff and others (2005); [2]Belnap and others (2009)

Transitions and Threshold Estimation

Based on every possible value of biological soil crust cover from 0 to 100 percent (at 0.5 percent intervals), aggregate stability and roughness were predicted from the values of biological soil crust cover, and magnetic susceptibility was predicted from the values of roughness (see equations in fig. 3). Finally, transition probabilities were predicted based on aggregate stability, surface roughness, and magnetic susceptibility. Thus for each of our critical probabilities (95 percent, 50 percent, 25 percent, 5 percent), we could simultaneously extract a set of values for biological soil crust, aggregate stability, surface roughness, and magnetic susceptibility. These values were: (1) soil aggregate stability: 4.7, 4.9, 5.0, and 5.17 (unitless scale from 0 to 6); (2) magnetic susceptibility: 0.10, 0.14, 0.16, 0.20×10^{-6} standard international units; (3) surface roughness: 5.4, 8.8, 10.5, 14.8 percent deviation from chain length [(1 – straight line distance from end to end of chain laid across a surface / length of chain) × 100]); and (4) biological soil crust cover: 7.5, 22.5, 30, 49.0 percent (fig. 4).

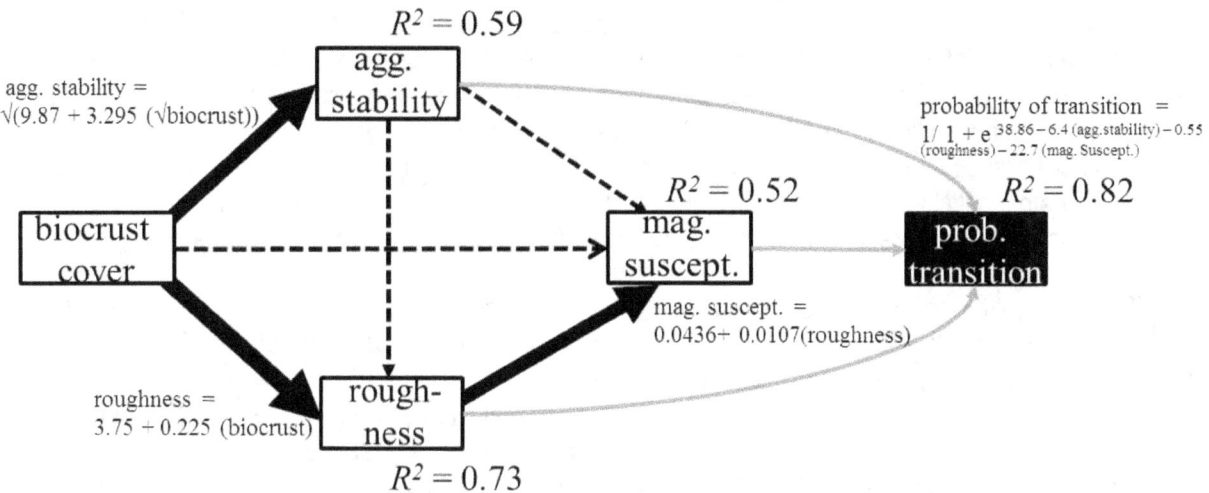

Figure 3. Path model showing a predictive framework integrating both linear regressions and logistic regressions to result in a state transition probability output. Boxes are measured variables. Arrows (paths) represent hypothesized causal relationships; dashed black paths did not enhance predictive capability, and were subsequently ignored; solid black arrows represent relationships retained and modeled using linear regressions, widths are scaled based on variance explained, regression equations are adjacent; and gray paths represent relationships retained and modeled using multiple logistic regression, regression equation is adjacent.

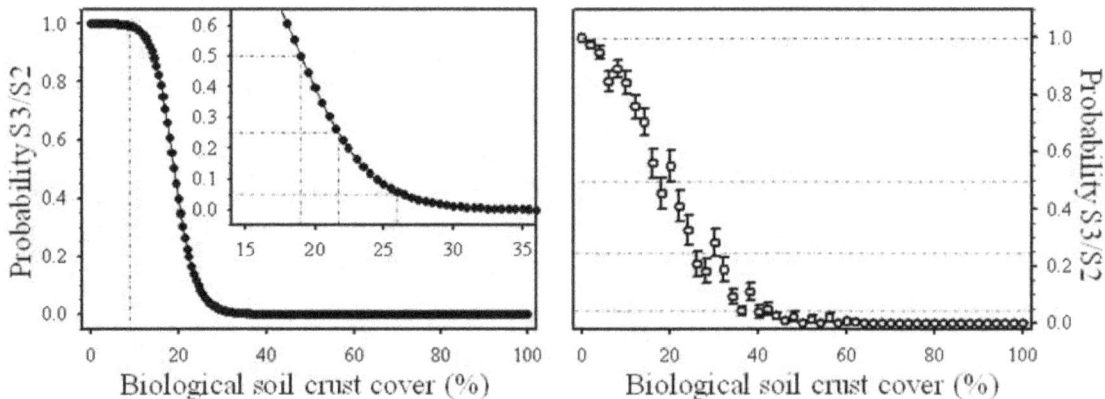

Figure 4. Path analysis-assisted multiple logistic regression models of the probability of transition from state 2 to 3, given the values of three variables (aggregate stability, surface roughness, magnetic susceptibility) which are linked by the common causal influence of biological soil crusts. The left graph represents the solution of the model across all possible values of biological soil crust values. Because the path model predicts the values of the predictors based on a causal model ultimately rooted in biological soil crust cover, the values of all three predictors increase as biological soil crust cover increases. The right graph depicts the outcome of the same model, simulated with a realistic level of stochasticity. Error bars represent the 95 percent confidence intervals of the outcome of 100 simulations. Dashed lines represent predicted critical probability values (5, 25, 50, and 95 percent).

The effect of stochasticity was to make the curve less steep (fig. 4). The mean simulated probability did not reach 100 percent, even at 0 percent biological soil crust cover. The point at which probability begins to diverge from zero occurs at higher biological soil crust values. The mean probability values most closely corresponding to our critical probability values are: 7.5 percent biological soil crust (95 percent probability), 22.5 percent biological soil crust (50 percent probability), 26.5 percent biological soil crust (25 percent probability), and 41 percent biological soil crust (5 percent probability). If we account for stochasticity and determine instead the 95 percent confidence interval surrounding transition probabilities for many levels of biological soil crust cover, different results are attained. Probability values of 25 percent were within the confidence intervals starting as low as 30 percent biological soil crust, and probability values of 5 percent were within the confidence intervals starting as high as 49.0 percent biological soil crust, owing to the stochasticity introduced into the model.

Our logistic regression analysis of the transition from S3 to S4 was "perfect" in that the pseudo R^2 was 1.0. Such functions are unstable because the logistic curve is so steep that the parameters are difficult to estimate. The precision of the estimates in this case is not important because the transition occurs abruptly between 26 and 27 percent relative exotic cover; pinpointing it further would not enhance our ability to detect a transition.

Interpretation

Biological soil crust abundance is strongly influenced by compressional disturbances, such as hoof action or human foot traffic. Climate also may play a role in dictating how much biological soil crust is present in a given year, and climate change may dictate the future trajectory of change especially in most national parks where compressional disturbances are tightly regulated. When considering the transitions from a biological soil crusted grassland to a grassland with bare interspaces, biological soil crust cover must remain high, and therefore bare ground must remain low, to ensure a less than 5 percent probability of transition. As biological soil crust cover is reduced to approximately 49 percent, transition becomes possible. If crust cover is then reduced to about 30 percent, transitions cease to be uncommon (25 percent probability). A very small further reduction to about 23 percent biological soil crust cover leads to equiprobability that a transition has or will occur. Finally, if biological soil crusts are allowed to decrease to about 7.5 percent then a transition almost certainly has occurred or will occur. A previous analysis of this data (Bowker and others, *in press*) suggested a tipping point of about 30 percent based on cover of bare ground, with assessment points falling between 20 and 30 percent. These two findings are complementary because when biological soil crust is lost it is replaced by bare ground.

The transition from grasslands with bare interspaces to annualized communities is much more abrupt and simple. All of the critical probabilities are between 26 and 27 percent. If exotic annuals compose more than 26 percent of the plant community, a transition has occurred or is imminent. This value corresponds reasonably well with a value of 28.3 percent based on classification trees (Bowker and others, *in press*). The NPS I&M network is well equipped to detect these changes because biological soil crusts, exotic annuals and bare ground are currently being monitored in multiple national parks with SDSL ecosystems.

Case Study 2: Mesa Top Pinyon-Juniper

Background

At Bandelier National Monument, ecological site mapping has not yet been completed. SCPN and park staff defined the Mesa top pinyon-juniper ecological site as a basis for the NPS I&M program work, based on landscape position and dominant vegetation (DeCoster and Swan, 2011). As suggested by the name, it was (until recently) characterized by open woodlands of *Pinus edulis* and *Juniperus monosperma*. Soils are a mosaic of material derived from rhyolitic tuffs, pumice, and some eolian-deposited material (Hibner, 2000). This ecological site has a complex history full of drastic changes. It is not easily ascribed a reference state. The area was densely populated by puebloan cultures from 1150 to 1550, and it is believed that the mesa tops were deforested (Allen, 2004). After centuries of recovery, sheep and cattle grazing occurred from the 1880s to 1932, followed by persistence of feral burros (Hastings and others, 2003). It is widely believed that because of grazing, a herbaceous groundstory was diminished, favoring higher density of trees and initiating soil erosion (Miller and Wigand, 1994; Brockway and others, 2002). It is also widely believed that the elimination of the herbaceous vegetation removed fire from the ecosystem (Allen, 2004). Even with the creation of the Bandelier National Monument and the retirement of grazing, high erosion rates continued possibly exacerbated by a drought in the 1950s (Davenport and others, 1998). Because of the erosion problem, it was thought that the mesa tops were in a persistent degraded state characterized by unsustainable erosion rates. This led managers to initiate both small- and large-scale manipulations based on selective thinning of mature trees and scattering the woody debris into eroding interspaces (Jacobs, 2002; Hastings and others, 2003). This practice led to a decrease in erosion rates and an impressive increase in herbaceous vegetation (Hastings and others, 2003). The landscape was highly altered by a drought in the first years of the current millennium (Breshears and others, 2005; Gitlin and others, 2006). This unusually warm drought killed about 90 percent of the mature *P. edulis* trees, largely leaving *Juniperus* woodlands. Some large scale restoration activities have occurred after the drought, taking advantage of dead trees, to redisperse woody debris to interspaces.

Method Details

A Priori State-and-Transition Models

Field observations, published literature, and discussion with NPS staff provided the basis for developing a STM articulating hypotheses about system dynamics, degradation pathways among alternative states, and associated ecosystem patterns, processes, and feedbacks. The conceptual model identifies six ecosystem states based on persistent differences in the relative abundance of biotic functional types. We omit prehistorical states because too little is known about them. We include a pre-grazing historical state but acknowledge that this also is poorly understood and that the ecosystem may have permanently transitioned away from this state.

Our *a priori* model hypothesizes a savanna ecosystem with an overstory of *P. edulis* and *J. monosperma*, characterized by occasional fire which prevents a thicketization (Jacobs, 2002). This state is not prone to high erosion rates. Introduction of grazers coupled with fire suppression leads to a more closed woodland state; this state is erodible, but is not actively eroding. From a woodland state, a nexus of an erodible soil surface and high water erosivity (propensity for water to move sediment) can lead to an actively eroding woodland state. Erosion prevents establishment of plants in the interspace. A crown fire in the woodland state is also likely to lead to a treeless, actively eroding state with compromised overstory and understory. Drought is a major force influencing various woodland states by causing tree mortality, especially in *P. edulis,* although *Juniperus* spp. are not immune (B. Jacobs, NPS, oral commun. 2011, Bowker and others, 2012b). A woodland may experience major mortality in the overstory, allowing an eventual release or "green-up" effect benefiting grasses and forbs and creating an open woodland with herbaceous understory. An actively eroding woodland also will lose trees due to drought, possibly transitioning into a treeless, actively eroding state. Restoration treatments consisting of removal of mature trees and dispersing slash throughout the interspace may transition woodlands or actively eroding woodlands into open woodlands or restored savannas with herbaceous interspaces and low erosion rates. Maintenance by fire may transition these ecosystems back to the reference savanna state.

Data

We focused our analysis on a 15-year dataset documenting a landscape-scale experiment (Hastings and others, 2003). The "paired watershed study" examines two adjacent watersheds draining the low elevation mesa tops in Bandelier National Monument. One watershed was selected for a treatment that consisted of removal of about 70 percent of the trees and dispersing the slash throughout the interspaces (Frijoles Mesa), whereas the other was left as an untreated control (Garcia Mesa). Each mesa was monitored along twenty 100-m line transects that ran from mesa tops downslope; each can be subdivided into upper and lower 50-m segments, and have been analyzed in this way in the past (Jacobs and others, 2002). This results in a sample size of 80 transects in total. The data include pre-treatment data from 1996, and capture an extreme drought that led to mass tree mortality. One-half of the thinned samples were subjected to an experimental prescribed fire in spring 2010. The transects were monitored annually from 1996 to 2000, and again in 2008 and 2010. Data collected include plant percent cover by species (separated into live and dead fractions) and ground cover. The strong spatial replication, temporal richness, and combination of imposed and unplanned ecosystem change make this an extremely high value dataset for this purpose.

Cluster Analyses

We validated and revised definitions of states and phases of our *a priori* state-and-transition model by conducting a hierarchical cluster analysis of both live and dead plant functional group cover (with the exception that *J. monosperma* and *P. edulis* were treated at the species level rather than using a tree functional group), rock cover, litter cover, downed wood cover, and bare ground cover. For the purposes of our analysis, we treated upper and lower sections of transects as unique observations (as previously done in published accounts of this experiment), and treated transect readings of different years as independent observations. The consequences of these simplifications are that it should be more difficult to ascribe the lower and upper segment of a transect, or transect observations in different years to separate clusters. This is because upper and lower segments will tend to resemble each other more than will different transects, and a single transect at a given time point will tend to be similar to itself at a different time point. Thus, from the standpoint of clustering data, this can be considered a conservative analysis. Nevertheless, in practice we had no difficulty ascribing different cluster membership to the same transect through time, or transect segments linked in space.

Based on the expected number of clusters in our *a priori* models (6), we examined results for 2–10 cluster solutions. Cluster analyses are subjective descriptive tools and should not be viewed as strict hypothesis tests. We used the following guidelines to select the best number of clusters: (1) acknowledging that we may not observe all of the clusters in our *a priori* model (and that their absence does not prove they do not exist), and that additional clusters may exist that we did not anticipate, we selected a solution with a number of clusters reasonably close to our prior expectations; (2) we accepted clusters which were a good match with our prior expectations, if they existed; (3) we accepted unanticipated clusters when they were consistent with a mechanistic explanation as to how they could emerge (for example dictated by abiotic factors or a likely outcome of a given disturbance); (4) we aimed for the number of clusters which explained about one-half the variation in the data. We selected the solution that *best* satisfied *all* of the above criteria. To help us define the characteristics of our clusters we applied indicator species analysis (Dufrene and Legendre, 1997) and viewed NMDS ordinations. Similar clusters were grouped as phases of states as an interpretive aid.

Temporal Dynamics

As an additional aid to the development of a final state and transition model, we tabulated cluster membership for each transect segment over time. This assisted us in determining which transitions were possible and which triggers (treatment, drought) were likely involved. Because interannual variation can lead a transect of one cluster to resemble another cluster temporarily (that is, not invoking a persistent transition), we focused on apparent shifts which were observed in more than one time point.

Modeling Transitions

Using a state-and-transition model with states and phases validated in empirical data, we focused on individual transitions from one state or phase to another. There were four state transitions for which we had sufficient data to model a state transition. We extracted samples which had undergone shifts in cluster membership and possibly state transitions. In the one case where it yielded a sufficient number of samples, we applied a strict protocol to ensure that we were using samples that had undergone a clear transition. This was the transition from productive woodlands to open canopied woodlands. We selected samples which had been in the productive woodlands clusters in 1996, and had belonged to the open woodlands cluster in 2010. To be included, the samples had to have either occupied the open woodlands cluster for at least the final two samplings consecutively, or occupied this cluster in 2010 and in at least two other years regardless if the years were consecutive. After culling the dataset to only these samples we selected the data for the final year in which the sample occupied the productive woodlands clusters and the first year in which the sample occupied the open woodlands cluster consistently. We were left with a dataset of pairs of before and after transition observations.

For three other transitions, this approach would have yielded too few samples for analysis. Instead, we applied a more liberal set of inclusion rules. For a given beginning and end state of interest, we extracted data for all samples that had occupied both states of interest during the span of sampling. We calculated the means of numerous variables for the beginning and end state for each sample.

In most cases, we hypothesized fairly simple transition mechanisms represented either as 3-variable path models, or more simply, multiple logistic regression models. We then used these equations to determine the values for the predictors at which the transition probability of interest was 5 percent, 25 percent, 50 percent, and 95 percent.

Results

Cluster Analysis

We selected an eight-cluster solution which largely confirmed our conception of ecosystems states (fig. 5), but revealed some common variants within those states. We found evidence of both productive and unproductive woodlands. Unproductive woodlands may be those undergoing accelerated erosion, although this is not known with certainty. Productive woodlands are characterized by high litter and two clusters: Cluster 1 has a higher ratio of *J. monosperma* to *P. edulis* than cluster 2. Unproductive woodlands are characterized by bare ground: Cluster 3 has a higher cover of shrubs and *J. monosperma* than cluster 4. Open woodlands, represented by cluster 5 exhibit some degree of herbaceous vegetation and high cover of dead *P. edulis*. Savannas are represented by 3 clusters: Cluster 6, 7, and 8 differ in the amounts of litter, and live and dead herbaceous cover.

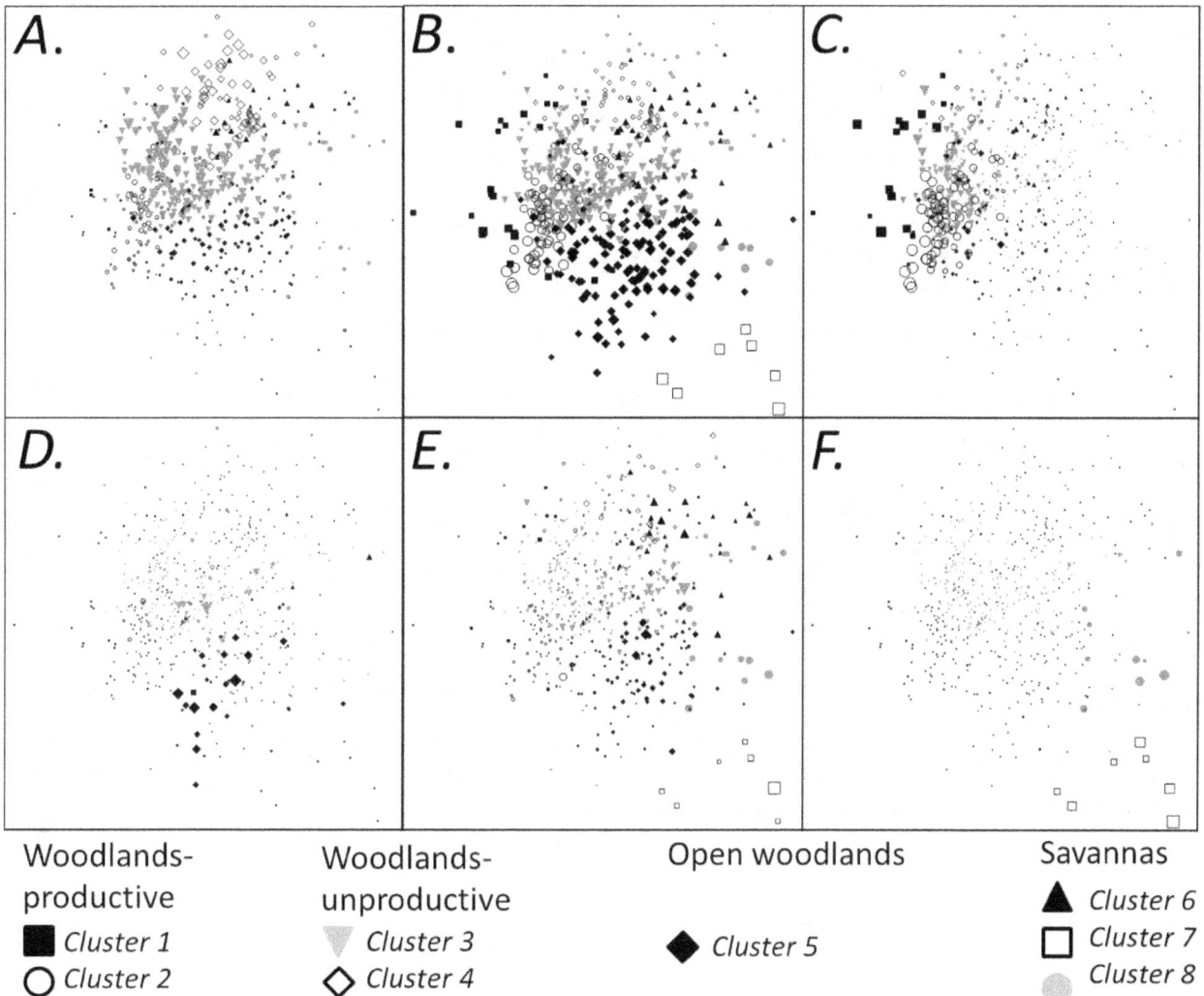

Figure 5. Diagrams showing six versions of an non-metric multidimensional ordination based on the eight-cluster solution. (*A.*) Symbols are scaled according to percent cover of bare ground, which is especially high in clusters 3 and 4. (*B.*) Symbols are scaled according to percent cover of litter, which is high in clusters 1, 2, 5 and 7. (*C.*) Symbols are scaled according to live *P.edulis* cover, which is high in clusters 1, 2, and to a lesser extent 3. (*D.*) Symbols are scaled according to dead *P. edulis* cover, which is high in cluster 5. (*E.*) Symbols are scaled according to live forb cover, which is high in clusters 6, 7 and 8. (*F.*) Symbols are scaled according to dead grass cover, which is high in cluster 7.

Temporal Analysis

An examination of cluster assignments of transect segments over time, in relation to known perturbations or manipulations, reveals much about possible transitions (table 2). For example, overall productive and unproductive woodlands prevail in similar numbers prior to treatment. Both treatment and drought lead to a greater prevalence of open woodlands over the course of monitoring. Treatment increases the prevalence of savannas. The effects of burning are unclear; in 50 percent of cases no state transition is observed.

Transitions from unproductive woodlands to open woodlands are observed, as are a few from unproductive woodlands to savannas. These apparent transitions come about from either an increase in litter retention or herbaceous cover (these transitions are short-lived or thus far not proven to persist). There is not a clear relationship of treatment or drought to these transitions. The most frequent outcome was for unproductive woodlands to remain unchanged, or move toward another state only to later regress.

A much clearer representation emerges for transitions from productive woodlands to open woodlands or savannas. Drought can suddenly transition a productive woodland into an open woodland, and does so in a majority of cases. Thinning can elicit the same response followed by transitions to savannas, or occasionally induce a lasting direct transition to savannas. Previously thinned transects are less obviously affected by subsequent drought.

Open woodlands appear to be an unstable state and can transition to savannas, especially under thinning, stay the same, or regress to unproductive woodlands.

Table 2. Cluster membership of samples through time.
[Clusters are color coded according to final state-and-transition model : red, unproductive woodlands; yellow, productive woodlands; blue, open woodlands; green, savannas]

	1996	1997 - 70% tree thinning	1997	1998	1999	2000	2001 - 2003 - extreme drought	2008	2010 - prescribed burn	2010
VC15U	3		3	3	3	3		3		3
VC18U	3		3	3	3	3		3		3
VC19U	3		3	3	3	3		3		3
VC20U	3		3	3	3	3	D	3		3
VC2U	3		3	3	3	3	R	3		3
VC18L	3		3	3	3	3	O	3		5
VC9L	3		3	3	3	3	U	3		5
VC1U	3		3	3	3	3	G	5		5
VC15L	3		3	3	3	3	H	4		4
VC19L	3		3	3	1	3	T	3		5
VC10L	3		3	5	3	3		3		3
VC12U	3		3	5	3	3		3		3
VC14U	3		3	5	3	3		3		3
VC9U	3		3	5	5	3	D	3		3
VC4U	3		3	5	5	3	R	3		5
VC11U	3		3	5	5	5	O	3		5
VC11L	3		3	1	1	3	U	3		3
VC17U	3		3	1	1	3	G	3		3
VT37L	3		3	3	5	3	H	3		3
VT33L	3		3	3	5	4	T	3	B	3
VT40L	3		3	5	5	3		3		5
VT38U	3		3	5	5	3		3		
VT34U	3	T	3	5	5	4		3	B	4
VT27U	3	H	3	6	5	4	D	3	B	4
VT36L	3	I	5	5	5	3	R	3		5
VT28U	3	N	5	5	5	5	O	3	B	3
VT35L	3	N	4	3	3	4	U	3	B	3
VT38L	3	I	4	3	5	4	G	3		3
VT32L	3	N	4	3	5	4	H	4	B	4
VT40U	3	G	4	5	3	3	T	4		3
VT31L	3		4	4	5	4		4	B	6
VT31U	3		4	6	5	4		4	B	3
VT24U	3		4	6	5	4		4		3
VT35U	3		4	6	5	4	D	4	B	4
VT34L	3		6	6	3	3	R	3		3
VT23U	3		6	6	5	4	O	6		8
VC7L	4		4	1	6	4		8		7
VT33U	4		3	5	5	4	D	3	B	4
VT37U	4	T	4	3	3	4	R	4		
VT32U	4	H	4	4	3	4	O	4	B	4
VT25U	4	I	4	4	5	4	U	8		8
VT27L	4	N	4	6	3	4	G	3	B	8
VT28L	4	N	4	6	3	6	H	8	B	8
VT30L	4		4	6	5	4	T	8	B	8

	1	2	3	4	5	6		7	8	9
VC20L	1		3	5	5	3	D	3		3
VC17L	1		1	1	5	1	R	5		5
VC12L	1		1	1	1	3	O	3		5
VC3U	1		1	1	1	3	U	5		5
VC13L	1		1	1	1	1	G	5		3
VC14L	1		1	1	1	1	H	5		5
VC16L	1		1	1	1	1	T	5		5
VC16U	1		1	1	1	1		5		5
VC4L	1		1	1	1	1		5		5
VC6U	1		1	1	1	1		5		5
VC8U	1		1	1	1	1		5		5
VC13U	1		1	1	1	1	D	5		
VC5U	1			1	1	1	R	5		5
VT24L	1	T	5	5	5	5	O	5		5
VT29U	1	H	5	5	5	5	U	6	B	5
VT30U	1	H	6	6	5	6	G	6	B	5
VT22U	1		6	6	5	6	H	8		7
VC7U	2		5	1	1	2	T	5		5
VC5L	2		1	1	1	3		6		5
VC8L	2		2	5	5	2		2		5
VC6L	2		2	5	2	2	D	2		5
VC3L	2		2	1	1	2	R	5		5
VC1L	2		4	5	5	4	O	5		5
VC2L	2		4	1	3	2	U	5		5
VT25L	2	T H	5	5	5	3	G	5		7
VT39L	2	H	5	5	5	3	H	2		5
VT23L	2	I	5	6	5	6	T	8		7
VT22L	2		1	6	5	6		8		7
VT29L	2		4	5	5	4		8	B	5
VT26L	2		6	6	5	6		8	B	7
VC10U	5		3	5	5	3	U	5		3
VT36U	5		3	5	5	3	G	3		3
VT39U	5	T H	5	5	5	3	H	5		5
VT26U	5	H	5	6	5	6	T	8	B	8
VT21U	5	I	4	6	5	6		8		8
VT21L	5		6	6	3	6		8		7

Final State-and-Transition Model

To a large degree, our *a priori* model was reasonably well-supported by the data. Three of the hypothesized states were confirmed and retained as states in the final model: Savannas, Open woodlands, and Unproductive woodlands (roughly equal to eroding woodlands in the *a priori* model). One hypothesized state (reference) was never observed, but its absence does not prove that it cannot exist, only that it was not observed, thus it is retained in the final state-and-transition model. One unanticipated difference between our *a priori* hypotheses and the observed clusters were the existence of productive and unproductive woodlands. We associated the latter with eroding woodlands that have been the target of restoration activities. We had conceived of the difference among eroding and non-eroding woodlands to be determined by erosive forces, however there were clear differences in tree productivity. Productive woodlands were in some cases associated with patches of high pumice accumulation, though not always. These revisions result in a state-and-transition model with five states and two phases each for productive and unproductive woodlands and three phases in the savannah state (fig. 6).

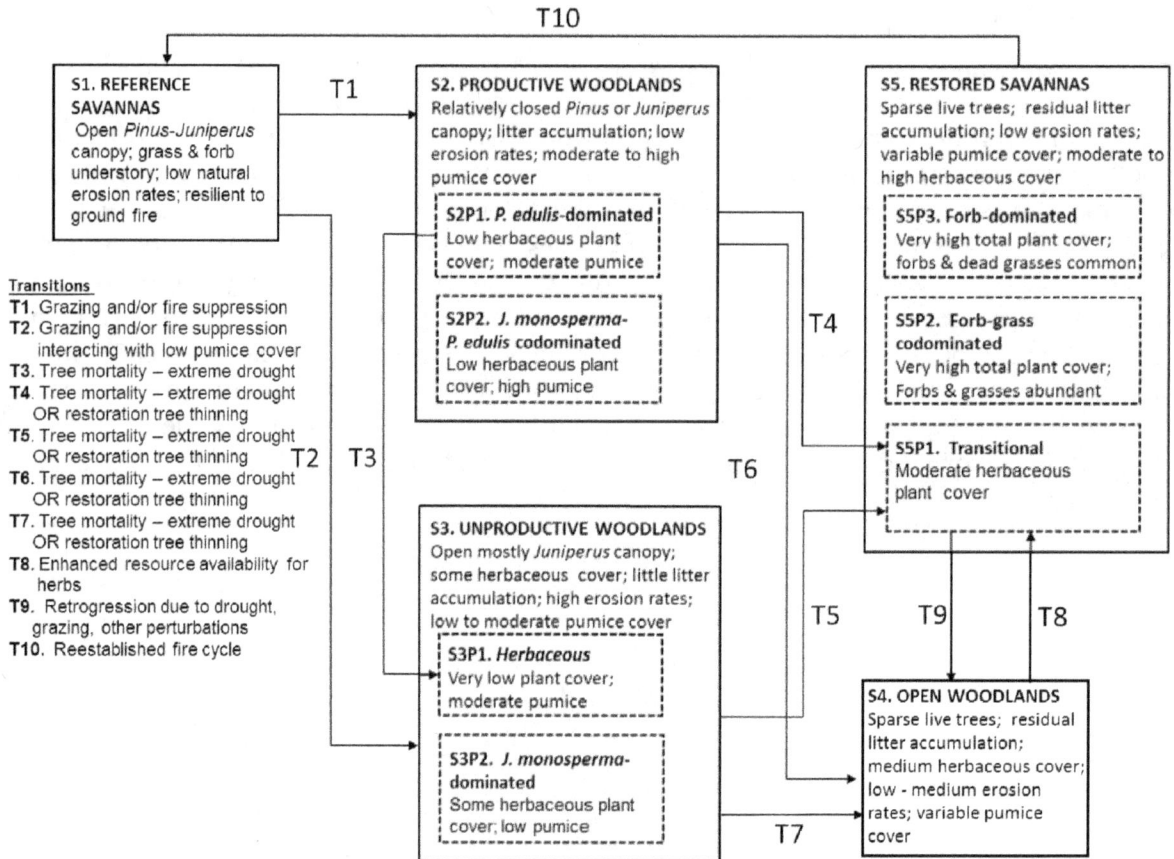

Figure 6. State-and-transition diagram for Mesa top pinyon-juniper. Solid boxes represent ecosystem states. Dashed boxes indicate phases within states. Arrows indicate transitions. In some cases, phases within the reference state are not connected to any others by arrows; this is our method of representing spatial variants of the reference state that are determined by abiotic factors, or cases where we simply do not have a strong hypothesis for the relationship among phases.

S1. Reference savannas: This state is not directly observed and may not currently exist within Bandelier. A similar state is assumed to have existed in the past as recently as the 19th century but is not clearly documented (Miller and Wigand, 1994). It also is a current desired ecosystem state and the target of restoration activities. This state would have a tree (*Pinus-Juniperus*) and herbaceous component. Overstory canopies are open. The state is expected to be resilient to low-intensity ground fire (Jacobs, 2002). Erosion rates are low. Understories may be composed of native grasses, forbs or a mixture.

S2. Productive woodlands: These woodlands are thought to be the result of past grazing. They are characterized by litter buildup on the soil surface and a higher density and canopy cover of either *J. monosperma* or *P. edulis*, or both. Because of the litter cover, these woodlands are less likely to be consistently eroding at accelerated rates. Shade and litterfall prohibits much herbaceous vegetation. The dichotomy between these productive woodlands and other unproductive woodlands (see S3) is probably partially related to spatial mosaics of pumice cover. Most extant productive woodlands have at least moderate and possibly high pumice cover (cluster means $\geq$ 17 percent).

S2Phase1*. P. edulis-*dominated: This phase is characterized by a *Pinus-Juniperus* overstory dominated by live *P. edulis* and has declined significantly in abundance after the 2001–03 drought. The existence of this phase is supported by cluster 1. *P. edulis* cover averages about 38 percent, and *J. monosperma* also is present. Summed herbaceous plant cover is the lowest of all clusters at 7 percent. Total cover is intermediate among clusters, but biomass is likely highest. Mean pumice cover is 17% percent.

S2 Phase2*. J. monosperma-P. edulis *codominated: This phase is characterized by a *Pinus-Juniperus* overstory dominated by live *J. monosperma* and is more resistant to change during drought. The existence of this phase is supported by cluster 2. This phase supports somewhat less litter and less summed plant cover (54 percent). *J. monosperma* and *P. edulis* are roughly equally represented with mean cover of 20 percent and 19 percent, respectively. Herbaceous cover is low and similar to the *P. edulis*-dominated Phase 1. Pumice cover is much higher than any other cluster at 53 percent.

S3. Unproductive woodlands: These woodlands are thought to be the result of past grazing and the subsequent initiation of accelerated erosion that tends to arrest ecosystem recovery (consistent with Davenport and others, 1998). They are characterized by bare soil surfaces and contain only depauperate woodlands or shrublands. Pumice cover is low to moderate (cluster means ≤ 16 percent).

S3 Phase 1. Herbaceous: This phase is characterized by overall low productivity. Summed plant cover is the lowest of any cluster at only 39 percent. Even *J. monosperma* and *P.edulis* attain only 5 percent cover or less. Moderate cover of herbaceous vegetation is common (24 percent).

S3 Phase 2*. J. monosperma-*dominated: In this phase, the bulk of the productivity is accounted for by *J. monosperma* (17 percent cover), and a modest summed herbaceous component (18 percent), mostly forbs.

S4. Open woodlands: This state is characterized by sparse live trees, either from drought mortality (Breshears and others, 2005; Gitlin and others, 2006) or restoration treatments (Jacobs, 2002; Hastings and others, 2003). Cluster 5 supports the existence of this state. In the case of the former, many may still be standing. In the case of the latter, tree debris has been redistributed across the site. The soil surface generally is not bare, but rather is covered by litter and supports some sparse understory of herbaceous vegetation. This state is not characterized by accelerated erosion. Live *P. edulis* cover is reduced to about 5 percent, whereas substantial *J. monosperma* cover remains (16 percent). Total summed cover is relatively low (57 percent), but compared to other woodland clusters, herbaceous cover is relatively high.

S5. Restored savannas: This state is composed of derived savannas, mostly from restoration activities. Live trees are sparse, and tree debris has been redistributed to interspaces. An understory of forbs and or grasses is common, some of which may be dead or senescent. The permanence of this state is unknown but several examples appear to have persisted for multiple years. This state is not characterized by accelerated erosion. Effects of fire are not yet fully known, but it appears that these derived savannas can often resist a state transition because of fire. These may become equivalent to S1 (Reference savannas) if they can withstand fires and maintain their savanna physiognomy, after the course woody debris has degraded. Exotic species likely compose a portion of the herbaceous understory.

S5 Phase 1. Transitional: This phase is supported by cluster 6. Tree cover is minor, averaging about 8 percent. Herbaceous cover is only slightly higher than some woodland states. The lack of dead herbaceous vegetation suggests that the herbaceous component is recently established. This interpretation is supported by the fact that most transects which eventually transition to the savanna state, initially occupy this phase (table 2).

S5 Phase 2. Forb-grass codominated: This phase is supported by cluster 7. Tree cover is the lowest of all clusters, yet summed total cover is the highest of all clusters at 81 percent. Live forbs and grasses are about equally represented, with summed cover of about 30 percent each.

S5 Phase 3. Forb-dominated: This phase is supported by cluster 8. Tree cover is again very low, and summed total cover high. The herbaceous vegetation is mostly forbs which are about 50 percent more abundant than live grasses. The cluster is characterized by relatively high amounts of dead grasses, suggesting accumulation of senescent material. An alternative explanation is that the grasses died during the drought.

Transitions and Threshold Estimation

Transition 6: S2. Productive woodlands to S4. Open woodlands: We selected live *P.edulis* as the primary determinant of membership in either the productive woodlands or open woodlands states. We screened properties of the understory and determined that live forbs was the one which most improved upon predictions made by live *P. edulis* alone. Because live *P. edulis* partially determines live forbs, we constructed a very simple path model (fig. 7*A*), wherein live forb cover was predicted as a linear function of proportional *P.edulis* cover ($R^2 = 0.35$), with a component of random error. Probability of transition was predicted as a logistic function of proportional cover of live *P. edulis* and live forbs. The pseudo R^2 of our predictive equation was 0.76. The equations were as follows:

$$\text{live forb cover} = -1.53-17.71 \text{ (live } P.\ edulis \text{ cover)} \qquad (1)$$

$$\text{probability of transition} = \qquad (2)$$

$$1/1 +e -(1.5379281-17.7095556 \text{ (live } P.\ edulis)+438.29148 \text{ (live forb cover))}$$

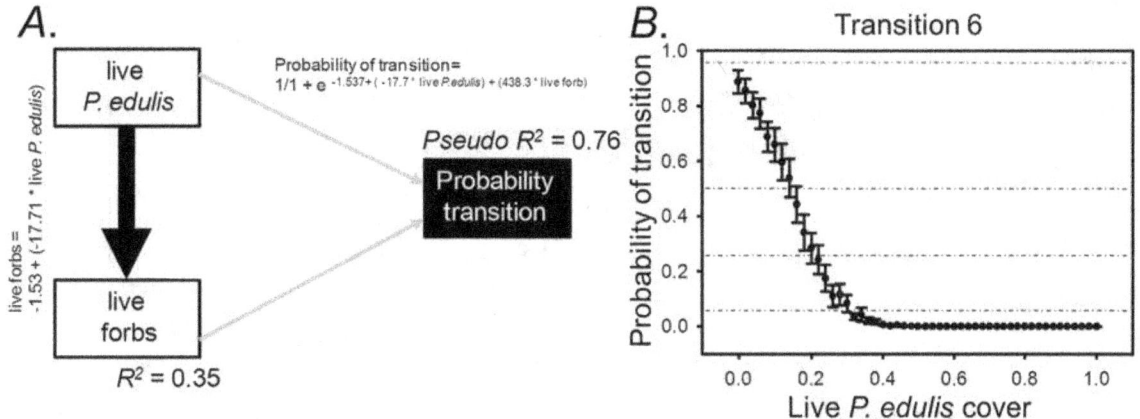

Figure 7. *A.* Path model articulating a predictive framework integrating both linear regressions and logistic regressions to result in a state transition probability output. Boxes are measured variables. Solid black arrows represent relationships modeled using linear regressions, widths are scaled based on variance explained, regression equations are adjacent; gray paths modeled using multiple logistic regression, regression equation is adjacent. *B.* Results of simulations based on the path model, illustrating critical probabilities of transition as a function of proportional *P. edulis* cover.

We solved for the proportional *P. edulis* cover required for a 5 percent, 25 percent, 50 percent, and 95 percent probability of transition (fig. *7B*). At proportional *P.edulis* cover of 0.34, a transition probability 5 percent becomes possible. A transition probability of 25 percent first becomes possible at 0.23. A transition probability of 50 percent first becomes possible at 0.16. Even if *P.edulis* cover is reduced to 0, a transition is not certain; the highest probability of transition observed was about 93 percent. Corresponding values of forb cover (0.005, 0.007, 0.009) are very low and would need to be measured very precisely. Nevertheless they help distinguish these clusters with more certainty.

Transition 7: S3. Unproductive woodlands to S4. Open woodlands: Because both states are characterized by low to medium tree cover, we screened key understory properties and selected litter as the primary determinant of membership in either the productive woodlands or open woodlands states. Accumulation of litter likely signals decreased erosion activity, and is thus a good indicator of transition to a more productive state. Bare ground was the variable which most improved upon predictions made by litter alone. Because litter partially determines bare ground, we constructed a very simple path model (fig. 8*A*), wherein bare ground was predicted as a linear function of proportional litter cover ($R^2 = 0.26$), with a component of random error. Probability of transition was predicted as a logistic function of litter and bare ground proportional cover. The pseudo R^2 of our predictive equation was 0.94. The equations were as follows:

$$\text{bare ground} = 0.52 - 0.497 \, (\text{litter cover}) \tag{3}$$

$$\text{probability of transition} = \tag{4}$$
$$1/1 + e - [17.76 - 94.27 \, (\text{bare soil}) + 86.5 \, \text{litter} \, (\text{litter})]$$

29

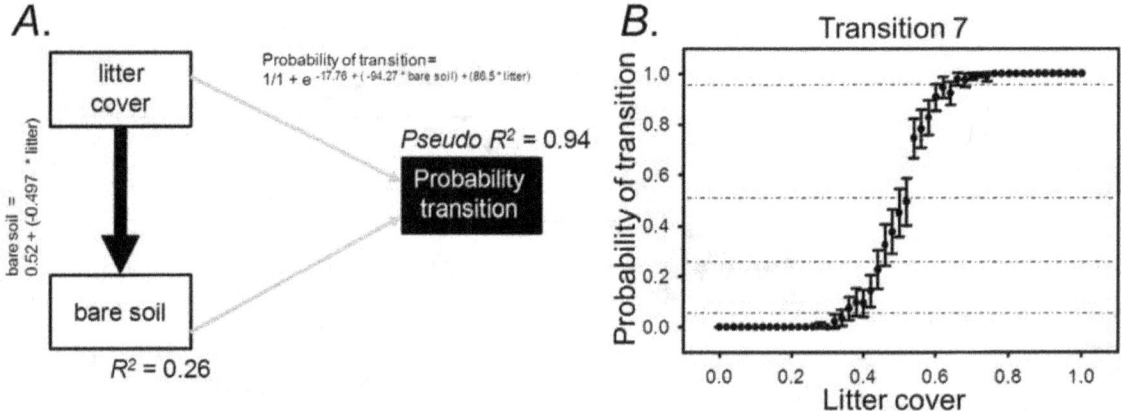

Figure 8. *A.* Path model articulating a predictive framework integrating both linear regressions and logistic regressions to result in a state transition probability output. Boxes are measured variables. Solid black arrows represent relationships modeled using linear regressions, widths are scaled based on variance explained, regression equations are adjacent; gray paths modeled using multiple logistic regression, regression equation is adjacent. *B.* Results of simulations based on the path model, illustrating critical probabilities of transition as a function of proportional litter cover.

We solved for the proportional litter cover required for a 5 percent, 25 percent, 50 percent, and 95 percent probability of transition (fig. 8*B*). These values become possible at litter cover of 0.33, 0.43, 0.49, and 0.60. Corresponding bare ground values were 0.36, 0.31, 0.28, and 0.23.

Transition 8: S4. Open woodlands to S5. Restored savannas: After screening several predictors primarily describing properties of the understory, we determined that the best parsimonious model was one with two predictors: total proportional cover of live and dead herbaceous plants (positively associated with S5 Restored savannas) and litter cover (negatively associated with S5 Restored savannas). These predictors were essentially uncorrelated, thus we did not use a path model to conserve their correlation structure. Including a variable indicating whether these plots had burned or not was not informative. We used a simple logistic regression model with the two predictors. The pseudo R^2 of our equation was 0.84. The equation was as follows:

$$\text{probability of transition} = \tag{5}$$
$$1/1+e-(12.09266+66.96835(\text{total live and dead herbaceous cover})-37.239(\text{litter cover}))$$

We solved for the total herbaceous proportional cover required for a 5 percent, 25 percent, 50 percent, and 95 percent probability of transition under proportional litter cover scenarios ranging from 0.1 to 0.9 in 0.05 increments (fig. 9). There are multiple combinations of herbaceous cover and litter cover that can produce these probabilities of transition.

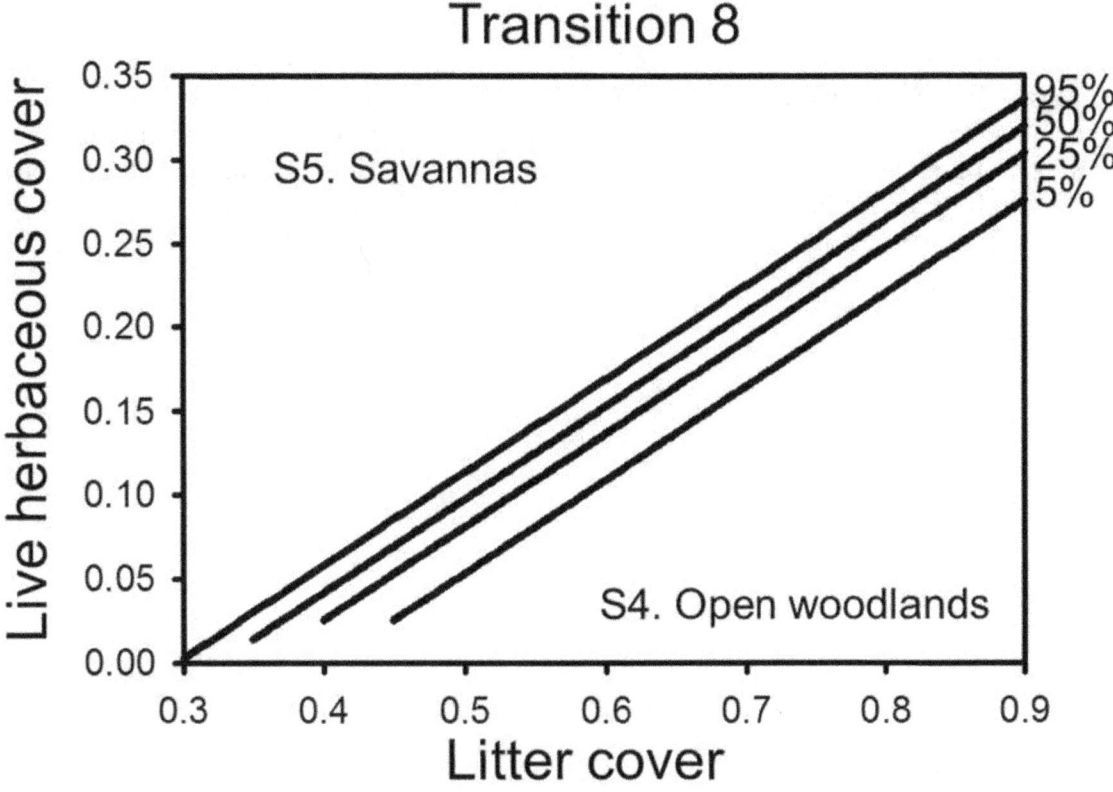

Figure 9. Graph showing critical probabilities of transition from open woodlands to savannas as determined by two key drivers.

Interpretation

With this ecological site we benefitted from having a dataset that was exceptionally rich temporally, and reasonable well-replicated spatially. This dataset illustrates the challenge of determining when a state transition has occurred definitively. We observed many cases where the same transect segment shifts back and forth among multiple clusters of data, which are considered roughly equivalent to phases. This suggests that transitions may move forward and backward in fits and starts. A shift from a multi-year apparent stable state to another multi-year stable state is our best approximation of a definitive state transition.

We were able to consider three transitions in detail, which together model indirect pathways from woodland states (some actively eroding) to derived savanna states, through a stable open woodland state. Although there would have been sufficient cases to also analyze the direct transition from unproductive woodlands to savanna, we do not have strong evidence that such a transition is commonly persistent. Many unproductive woodlands resemble other states or phases at single time points but revert back to unproductive woodlands.

The more likely pathway from unproductive woodlands to savannas is through transition 7, followed by transition 8. Our data suggest that these transitions can be detected in monitoring data by the buildup of litter resources (and consequent decline of bare ground), and its subsequent replacement by total live and dead herbaceous cover. To make this transition sequence nearly certain, management should allow or promote litter buildup to 0.6, and a reduction of bare ground to about 0.23. There are multiple combinations of litter cover and total live and dead herbaceous cover which regulate the next transition (fig. 9)

Of the transitions modeled, we have the highest confidence in transition 6, the pathway from productive woodlands to open woodlands. The data were edited to include only cases which convincingly had undergone persistent directional transitions. This transition can be brought about equally well by drought that kills *P. edulis*, or treatments involving thinning and slash redistribution. This transition can be detected in monitoring data by measuring live *P. edulis* cover and live forb cover. Subsequently, transition 8 may occur and be detected as described above.

Case Studies 3 and 4: Desert Shallow Sandy Loam (blackbrush) and Semidesert Shallow Sandy Loam (Utah juniper and pinyon pine)

Background

Desert and Semidesert shallow sandy loam ecological sites share many of the same dominant species, similar soils, and similar landscape settings. Accordingly, the alternative states and transitions among them are similar in the two ecological sites. Therefore, they are treated together in this chapter.

The NRCS does not have a published ecological site description for desert shallow sandy loam (blackbrush), as it is currently being revised. However, based on the preceding range site characteristics in Natural Resources Conservation Service (1991) the vegetation of this ecological site is more than one-half composed by *Coleogyne ramosissima*, with *Pleuraphis jamesii*, *Achnatherum hymenoides*, *Atriplex confertifolia*, *Ephedra torreyana*, and *Gutierrezia sarothrae* all being minor community components. NCPN used a spatial predictive model to determine the spatial extent of this ecological site, while awaiting the completion of a current soil survey (Witwicki, 2009a). The NRCS does have a draft ecological site description posted for semidesert shallow sandy loam (Utah juniper-pinyon pine) (ftp://ftp-fc.sc.egov.usda.gov/UT/Range/D35XY/035XY236UT.pdf). The ecological site description indicates a soil primarily derived from eolian depositon of weathered sandstone. Soils may be as shallow as 10–20 in. to bedrock. The vegetation is dominated by shrubs, primarily *Coleogyne ramosissima*, with *Ephedra torreyana* and *Artemisia bigelovii* as sub-dominants. *Juniperus osteosperma* and *Pinus edulis* may combine for about 20 percent cover. The description suggests that grasses have the potential to compose about 20 percent of the community, mostly represented by *Achnatherum hymenoides* and *Pleuraphis jamesii*. Biological soil crusts are considered minor ecosystem components in the ecological site description. The ecological site description indicates that *A. hymenoides, Hesperostipa comata*, and *A. bigelovii* decrease in response to grazing, whereas *C. ramosissima, P. edulis, J. osteosperma, Opuntia* spp., and *P. jamesii* increase.

Method Details

A Priori State-and-Transition Models

For both ecological sites, semidesert shallow sandy loam and desert shallow sandy loam, we envisioned a three-state concept. We envisioned a reference state with two phases. The first phase is the ungrazed ecosystem which would be shrub dominated, and contain a maximal amount of herbaceous palatable vegetation such as *A. hymenoides*. We also expected a biological soil crust component in this phase, suspecting that the potential importance of biological soil crusts had been underestimated in the ecological site description. The second phase of the reference state was envisioned as a grazing-impacted community with declining herbaceous and palatable vegetation in general, increased proportional abundance of unpalatable woody plants, and diminished biological soil crusts. The second state was hypothesized to emerge from the grazing-impacted phase of the reference state and to be strongly invaded by exotic annuals such as *Bromus tectorum*, creating a major annual component of the vegetation after grazing facilitated its establishment. The third state was hypothesized to be a severely eroded state which could develop from state 1 because of continued overstocking. In this state, palatable vegetation is expected to be denuded, biological soil crusts absent, overall plant cover reduced, and evidence of ongoing erosion evident.

Data

We analyzed a total of 164 samples for Semidesert shallow sandy loam and 40 samples representing Desert shallow sandy loam.

Semidesert shallow sandy loam samples originated from five sources:

- Grand Staircase-Escalante National Monument Rangeland Health dataset (1 sample) (Miller, 2008);
- NPS I&M plots of Canyonlands National Park (20 samples) (Witwicki, 2009a);
- Capitol Reef Vegetation Map Dataset (39 samples) (Clark and others, 2009);
- A rangeland assessment of Salt Creek Canyon and the Dugout Ranch, in and around Canyonlands National Park (33 samples) (Bowker and others, 2012a); and
- Arches vegetation mapping effort (71 samples) (Coles and others, 2009).

The desert shallow sandy loam samples originated from three sources:

- Grand Staircase-Escalante National Monument Rangeland Health dataset (5 samples) (Miller, 2008);
- Canyonlands Inventory and Monitoring dataset (18 samples) (Witwicki, 2009a); and Canyonlands vegetation map dataset (17 samples).

Cluster Analyses

We validated and revised our *a priori* state-and-transition models by conducting a hierarchical cluster analysis of vegetation community composition at the species level and biological soil crust cover. We lacked functional information on these ecosystems for most samples, thus chose to use the richest structural data we had in our cluster analyses. To standardize the various datasets collected by different observers using different techniques, we applied two steps. For step 1, removal of rare species was conducted, because these species are so infrequent they primarily introduce noise. We removed all species with less than five occurrences in semidesert shallow sandy loam and all species with less than three occurrences in the Desert shallow sandy loam; the differing criteria defining rareness indicates a greater sample size in semidesert shallow sandy loam. Finally, we omitted species represented by less than 10 total observations in either ecological site (for example, 5 occurrences in semidesert shallow sandy loam and 3 in desert shallow sandy loam would permit retention by the previous criteria but be omitted based on this one). For step 2, we applied a double relativization transformation. First, each column (a species) was rescaled from 0 to 1. Second, each row was rescaled from 0 to 1. This equalized the influence of each column, then purged the influence of total abundance in the sample.

Based on the expected number of clusters in our *a priori* models (three), we examined results for two to eight cluster solutions. Cluster analyses are subjective descriptive tools and should not be viewed as strict hypothesis tests. We used the following guidelines to select the best number of clusters: (1) based on threshold theory, that intermediates between states are unstable and would be uncommonly observed, we chose a number of clusters which displayed a low degree of overlap in ordination space; (2) acknowledging that we may not observe all clusters in our *a priori* model (and that their absence does not prove they do not exist), and that additional clusters that we did not anticipate may exist, we selected a solution with a number of clusters reasonably close to our *a priori* expectations; (3) we accepted clusters that were a good match with our *a priori expectations*, if they existed; and (4) we accepted unanticipated clusters when they were consistent with a mechanistic explanation as to how they could occur (for example, determined by abiotic factors or a likely outcome of a given disturbance). We selected the solution that *best* satisfied *all* of the above criteria. To help us define the characteristics of our clusters, we applied indicator species analysis (Dufrene and Legendre, 1997), and viewed NMDS ordinations. As an additional interpretational aid, we maximized correlation with time since grazing on axis 1 of the NMDS ordination. We updated our state-and-transition concept based on the results of the cluster analysis.

Modeling Transitions

Equipped with a state-and-transition model with states and phases validated in empirical data, we focused on individual transitions from one state or phase to another. There was only a single state transition for which we had sufficient data to model a state transition, where the reference ecosystems (a phase relatively rich in grasses) make the transition to an annualized state (see final state-and-transition model below). The preceding cluster analysis was used to assign samples to clusters corresponding to these designations. We used the NCPN integrated dataset to extract 46 samples representing either the reference (grassy phase) or annualized states. We focused our modeling efforts on the following data: (1) currently grazed (binary) as an indication of recent disturbance regime, (2) biological soil crust cover as an indicator of recent disturbance regime and resistance of soil surface to exotic annual establishment, (3) total plant cover as an index of recent consumption of forage and competitive barriers to the establishment of exotic annuals, (4) relative cover of exotic annuals as an index of the degree of invasion, standardized by the site productivity, and (5) state membership. We developed a path model to articulate our hypothesis about how this transition may occur. Total plant cover and crust cover were well predicted by simple linear regressions using grazing as a predictor, after data transformation. Relative cover of exotic annuals was modeled as a linear function of grazing, crust cover, and total plant cover. This was a full factorial model in which the second order interactions were particularly important in this predictive equation. State membership was predicted as a multiple logistic function of relative cover of exotic annuals, with contributions from biological soil crust cover and total plant cover.

We parameterized each of these equations. We solved this system of equations, in the "upstream" to "downstream" sequence as defined by the path model to simulate data with the correlative structure of the real data. In order to simulate a wide variety of combinations of the predictors of probability of transition, we solved the system of equations, with error, for continuous grazing values ranging from 0 to 1, at a resolution of two decimal places. Although, in the real data, grazing is a binary variable; it is easy to envision a continuous grazing intensity underlying this coarse indicator. We solved this system of equations 100 separate times and calculated a mean probability and 95 percent confidence interval for each level of grazing. We determined the lowest grazing level at which probability of transition was 25 percent and 50 percent. Normally, we would do so for 5 percent and 95 percent, but a grazing intensity of 0 resulted in probability greater than 5 percent, and a grazing intensity of 1 resulted in probability less than 95 percent.

Other transitions were not easily modeled. However, in clusters with a high potential for biological soil crusts, we demonstrated the variation in biological soil crust cover and its functional significance. Using the sites within blackbrush shrubland or wooded shrubland clusters (see details in *Cluster Analysis: Semidesert Shallow Sandy Loam*), we used the NCPN database to plot linear regressions of soil stability as a function of biological soil crust cover. In the database, there were seven samples of blackbrush shrublands with soil stability and biological soil crust measurements for the desert shallow sandy loam ecological site. There were 21 samples of blackbrush shrublands for semidesert shallow sandy loam. There were 18 samples of wooded shrublands in the semidesert shallow sandy loam ecological site with the appropriate data. We used the square of the soil stability value because the data generated by the Herrick soil stability test (Herrick and others, 2001) is curvilinearly related to continuous measures of aggregate stability; the transformation helps linearize the scale. We

35

prepared four different regressions: (1) Semidesert shallow sandy loam wooded shrublands, (2) Semidesert shallow sandy loam blackbrush shrublands, (3) Semidesert and Desert shallow sandy loam blackbrush shrublands, and (4) all of the above, combined. The Desert shallow sandy loam blackbrush shrublands were not replicated well enough to be considered on their own, thus we pooled them with similar sites from *Semidesert* shallow sandy loam to generate regression 3. Because regressions 1–3 were strikingly similar, we also pooled all data and generated a regression for all simultaneously.

Results

Cluster Analysis: Semidesert Shallow Sandy Loam

Because of much better replication, we analyzed Semidesert sandy loam first. We selected a five-cluster solution (fig. 10). Our ordination was three-dimensional. Most clusters separated relatively cleanly, although viewing all three axes is necessary to see the separation. Some clusters did tend to separate based on time since grazing, whereas other distinctions appeared unrelated.

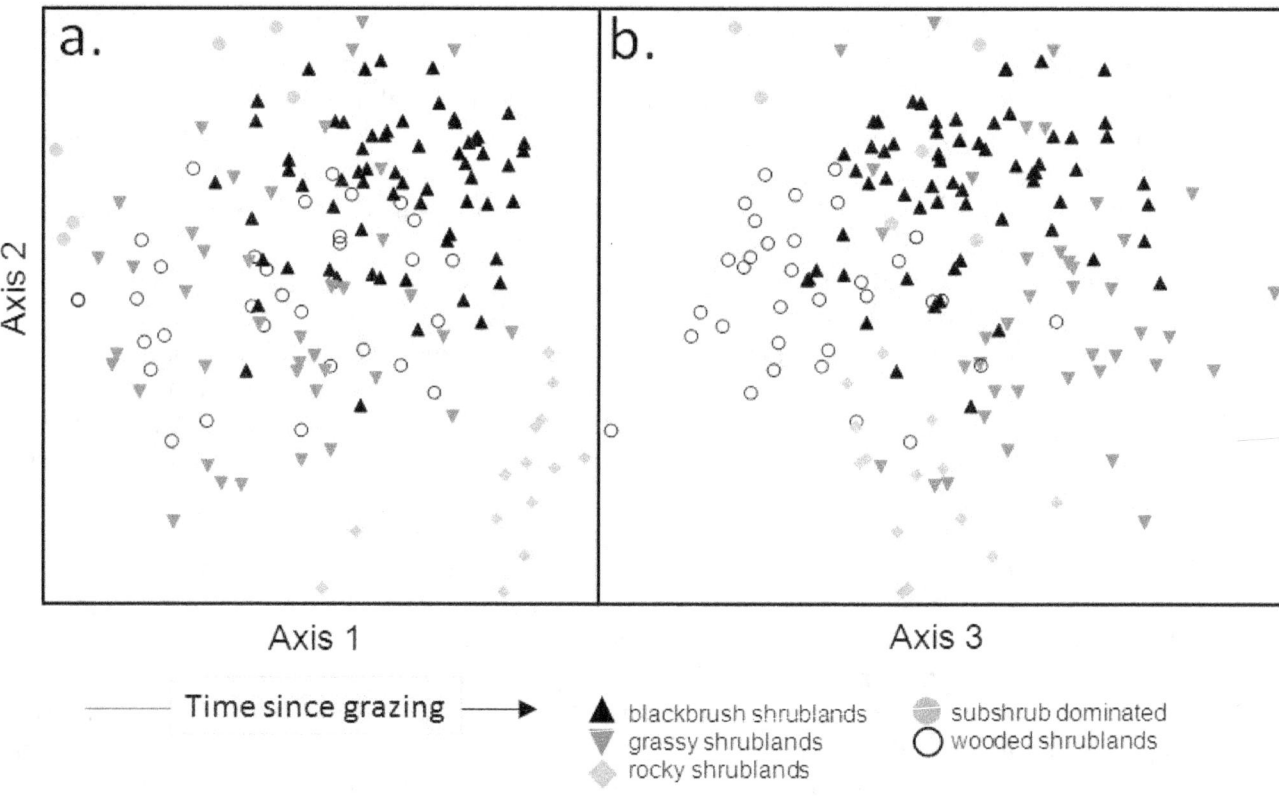

Figure 10. Non-metric multidimensional scaling ordination of a five-cluster solution in three-dimensions. (a) Most clusters separate well when viewing the two strongest axes (the horizontal axis is rotated to maximize correlation with time since grazing), with the exception of a wooded shrubland cluster. The annualized cluster is best correlated with current or recent grazing. (b) A view of the first and third axes demonstrates that the wooded shrublands also separate from the other clusters.

Based on the five-cluster solution, we determined the degree of correlation of various species with the clusters (fig. 11). We determined there were clusters indicated by: (1) biological soil crusts (indicators of two clusters, both positively related to time since grazing; (2) *Chrysothamnus viscidiflorus* (indicator of one cluster positively related to time since grazing but not overlapping with biological soil crusted clusters); (3) *C. ramosissima* (indicator of one cluster, positively related to time since grazing and overlapping with biological soil crusts); (4) *P. edulis* (indicator of one cluster, associated with moderate time since grazing and associated with biological soil crusts); 5. *Opuntia* spp. (indicator of one cluster, negatively related to time since grazing); and (6) *A. hymenoides* (indicator of one cluster, associated with moderate time since grazing).

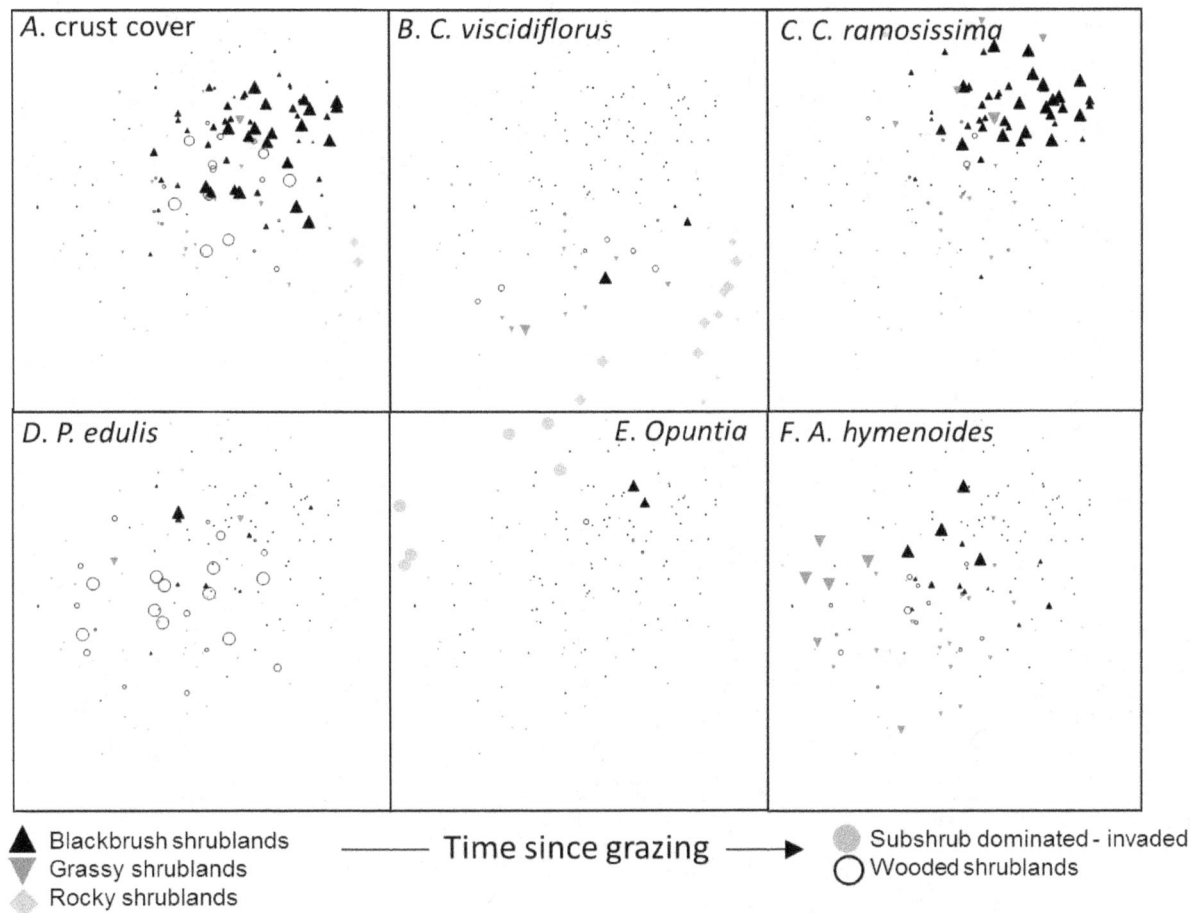

Figure 11. Six versions of non-metric multidimensional scaling ordination illustrating indicator species of the various clusters. In each panel, the symbols are resized based on the abundance of a single species or biotic component. It is clear that particular species correlate well with particular clusters: (A) Biological soil crust cover, an indicator of blackbrush and wooded shrublands. (B) *C. viscidiflorus*, an indicator of rocky shrublands. (C) *C. ramosissima*, an indicator and namesake of blackbrush shrublands. (D) *P. edulis*, an indicator of wooded shrublands. (E) *Opuntia*, an indicator of annualized. (F) *A. hymendoides*, an indicator of grassy shrublands.

Final State-and-Transition Model: Semidesert Shallow Sandy Loam

One of the hypothesized states (annualized) was confirmed and retained as a state in the final model. One hypothesized state (severely eroded) was never observed, but its absence does not prove that it cannot exist, only that it was not observed, thus it is retained in the final state-and-transition model. The other hypothesized state, the reference, was determined to be much more variable than we had anticipated. Multiple dominant shrubs, presence of trees, and a surprising prevalence of grasses in some plots were patterns not easily explained by grazing. We discovered a need to incorporate spatial variation due to abiotic factors in addition to grazing-induced vegetation changes such as the loss of biological soil crusts. We therefore interpreted grassy shrublands (indicated by *A. hymenoides*) and rocky shrublands (indicated by *C. viscidiflorus*) as spatial phases of the reference state which appear to be determined by differences in soil depth and degree of surface rock cover. The low disturbance phase of our hypothesized reference state proved to be two distinct clusters with differing proportions of *C. ramosissima* and *P. edulis*, apparently determined by precipitation. These were reinterpreted as distinct spatial phases of the reference state, wooded shrublands and blackbrush shrublands. In both of these clusters there is a gradient of biological soil crust cover corresponding to time since grazing. Thus, unlike some other ecological sites in this report, distinct states lacking biological soil crusts were not supported by our analysis.

These revisions result in a three-state, state-and-transition model with six phases of the reference state (fig. 12). Three of these phases are at-risk and potentially subject to transition out of the reference state.

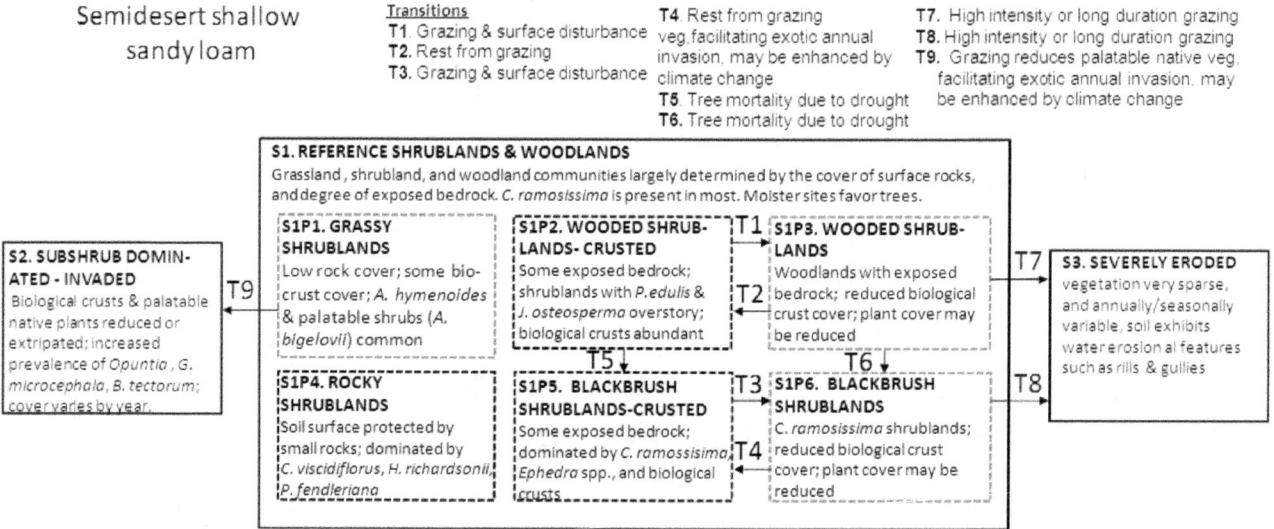

Figure 12. State-and-transition diagram for semidesert shallow sandy loam. Solid boxes represent ecosystem states. Dashed boxes indicate phases within states (red signifies a phase that is at-risk of transition to another state). Arrows indicate transitions. In some cases, phases within the reference state are not connected to any others by arrows; this is our method of representing spatial variants of the reference state that are dictated by abiotic factors.

S1. Reference shrublands and woodlands: Multiple distinct vegetative communities can be observed. They appear to largely be determined by abiotic factors rather than disturbance and successional processes. Soil depth and proportion of the surface covered by rocks seem to dictate dominant vegetation, and biological soil crust cover (as rock increases, the amount of available habitat for crusts decreases). Most of the reference communities contain *C. ramosissima*. Sites with low to moderate surface rock, and shallow depth (indicated by exposures of bedrock) tend to favor *C. ramosissima* shrublands or *Pinus-Juniperus* woodlands. Their relative prevalence is likely influenced by regional factors such as precipitation, and local factors such as bedrock fissures for rooting.

S1 Phase1. Grassy shrublands: This phase is characterized by few exposures of bedrock, and low levels of surface rock. Such sites are dominated by the grass *Achnatherum hymenoides*, and palatable shrubs such as *A. bigelovii* or *Eriogonum corymbosum*. It can be inferred that soils are relatively deep compared to other phases. In a low-disturbance state, biological soil crust cover is frequent but modest, usually 5–10 percent. This phase may be invaded by *B. tectorum*, but it is not a major component.

S1 Phase2. Wooded shrublands – crusted: This phase is characterized by low surface rock cover and shallow soils indicated by bedrock exposures. *J. osteosperma* and/or *P. edulis* are characteristic of this phase along with various shrubs including *C. ramosissima*, *Shepherdia rotundifolia*, *Mahonia fremontii*, *Ephedra viridis* and *Artemisia tridentata*. Such sites with high available habitat and possibly perched water, have a high propensity to support biological soil crusts with cover often reaching 15 percent or S3 Severely eroded.

S1 Phase3. Wooded shrublands: This phase is identical to S1P2 (Wooded shrublands-crusted), except that biological soil crust cover has been compromised by surface disturbances. Total plant cover may be reduced. Invasion by *B. tectorum* is uncommon and of minor severity.

S1 Phase4. Rocky shrublands: This phase is characterized by surfaces dominated by small rocks. The vegetative community is quite distinct, being dominated by *C. viscidiflorus* and *Hymenoxys richardsonii*. *Poa fendleriana* is the most common palatable species. Biological soil crusts are uncommon, as there is little available habitat. This is because, by definition, biological soil crusts inhabit soil, and rock cover reduces soil cover. Invasion by *B. tectorum* is uncommon and of minor severity.

S1 Phase5. Blackbrush shrublands – crusted: This phase is characterized by low surface rock cover, and shallow soils indicated by bedrock exposures. The vegetation is naturally dominated by *C. ramosissima* and *Ephedra* spp. Such sites with high available habitat and possibly perched water have a high propensity to support biological soil crusts with cover often reaching 20 percent or greater. Invasion by *B. tectorum* is uncommon and of minor severity.

S1 Phase6. Blackbrush shrublands: This phase is identical to S1P4 (Blackbrush shrublands-biological soil crusted), except that biological soil crust cover has been compromised by surface disturbances. Total plant cover may be reduced. Invasion by *B. tectorum* is uncommon and of minor severity.

S2. Subshrub dominated - invaded: Based on physical attributes (relatively low exposed bedrock and surface rock) and some floristic similarities, we suggest this state is likely to occur from grazing disturbance to S1P1 (grassy shrublands). It is dominated by native unpalatable shrubs such as *Gutierrezia* and *Opuntia* spp. Additionally, *B. tectorum* may be a major community component, even codominating. Because of the potentially high contribution of *B. tectorum* to total cover, inter- and intraannual variation in total cover is possible. Biological soil crusts are typically eliminated or occur in low abundance.

S3. Severely eroded: This state is largely theoretical. When a site is naturally lacking in surface rocks, its soil erodibility can be increased by loss of biological soil crusts (this occurs previously in the transition from wooded shrublands-crusted to ooded shrublands, and from Blackbrush shrublands - crusted to blackbrush shrublands). Erosivity, the ability of erosive forces to move sediment, is largely modified by properties of the plant community. When erodibility and erosivity are high, erosion is certain to occur. If grazing intensity or drought mortality (or other disturbance such as ORVs and seismic explorer rigs, etc.) is so great that the erosivity-dampening properties of the vegetative community are degraded, a positive feedback may be initiated whereby erosion prevents vegetation recovery.

Cluster Analysis: Desert Shallow Sandy Loam

In the case of Desert shallow sandy loam, we selected a three-cluster solution (fig. 13). All clusters separated very cleanly, suggesting distinct states.

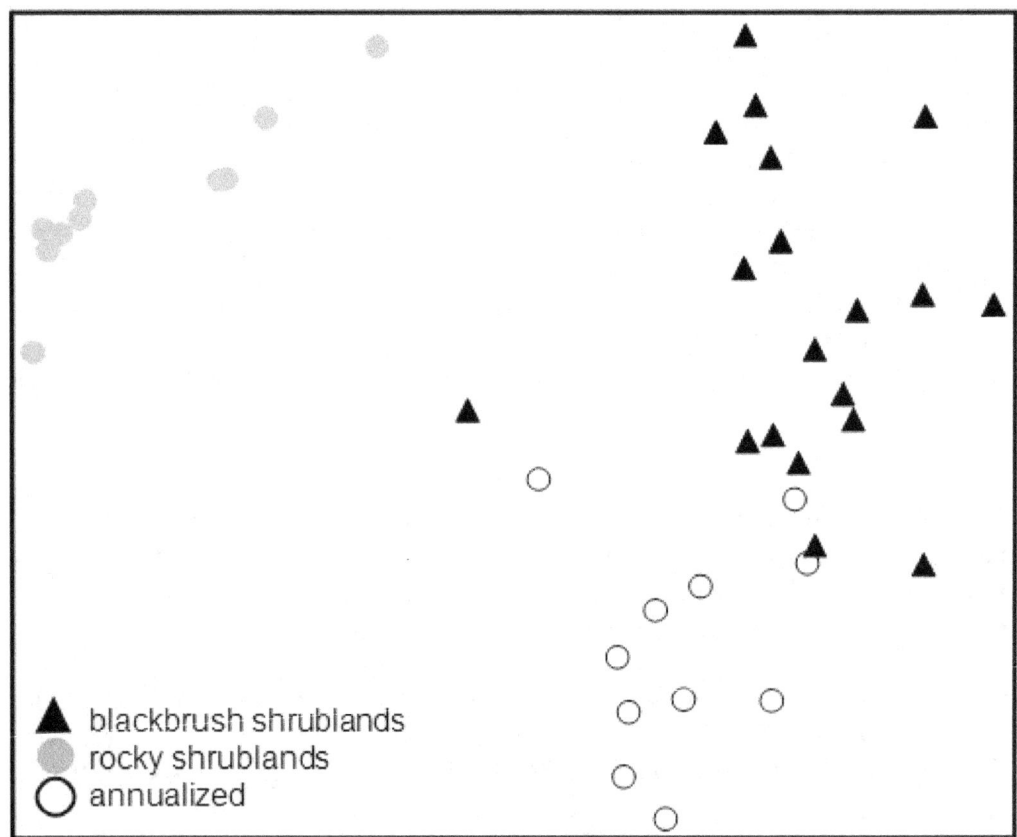

Figure 13. Non-metric multidimensional scaling ordination of a three-cluster solution.

Based on the three-cluster solution, we determined the degree of correlation of various species with the clusters (fig. 14). We found there were clusters indicated by: (1) *C. ramosissima*, (2) *C. viscidiflorus*, and (3) *G. sarothrae*.

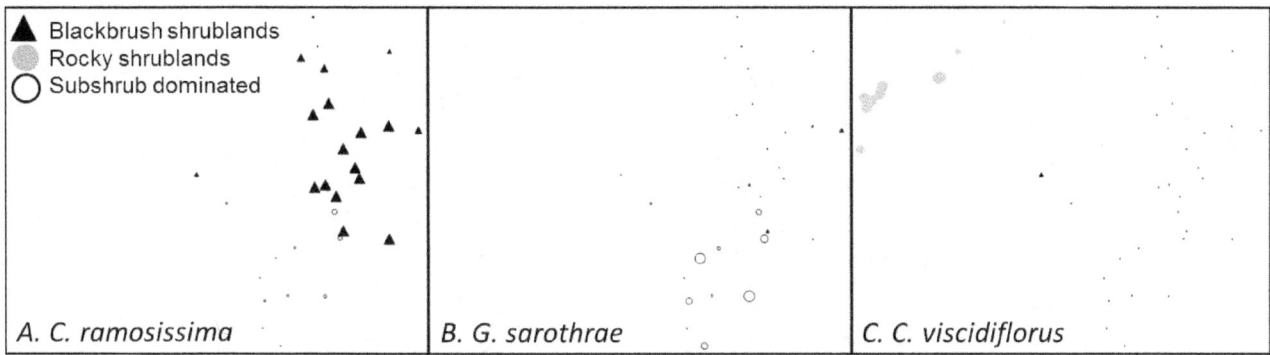

Figure 14. Three versions of non-metric multidimensional scaling ordination showing indicator species of the three clusters. In each panel, the symbols are resized based on the abundance of a single species or biotic component. It is clear that particular species correlate well with particular clusters. (*A*) *C. ramosissima*, an indicator and namesake of blackbrush shrublands. (*B*) *C. viscidiflorus*, an indicator of rocky shrublands. (*C*) *G. sarothrae*, an indicator of the annualized state.

Final State-and-Transition Model: Desert Shallow Sandy Loam

Using our *a priori* model and knowledge gained from our analysis of semidesert sandy loam we revised our state-and-transition model for desert shallow sandy loam (fig. 15). As with semidesert sandy loam, one hypothesized state (annualized) was observed and confirmed (best indicated in this case by *G. sarothrae* rather than *Opuntia* spp.), and another (severely eroded) was not observed but retained as a possibility in the final model. Because this ecological site is drier, there was no distinction between wooded shrublands and blackbrush shrublands, only blackbrush shrublands occurred. We also observed a cluster strongly reminiscent of the rocky shrublands identified in semidesert shallow sandy loam. Finally, we did not observe a phase corresponding to grassy shrublands, but based on its presence in semidesert sandy loam and its floristic similarities with the annualized state, we infer its existence as a precursor to annualized states. The sample size was considerably lower (40), only about one-half were not currently disturbed, thus it is entirely reasonable that such a phase exists but was not detected. Although biological soil crusts were much less prevalent in this ecological site, we retained a distinction between biological soil crusted and non-crusted blackbrush shrublands.

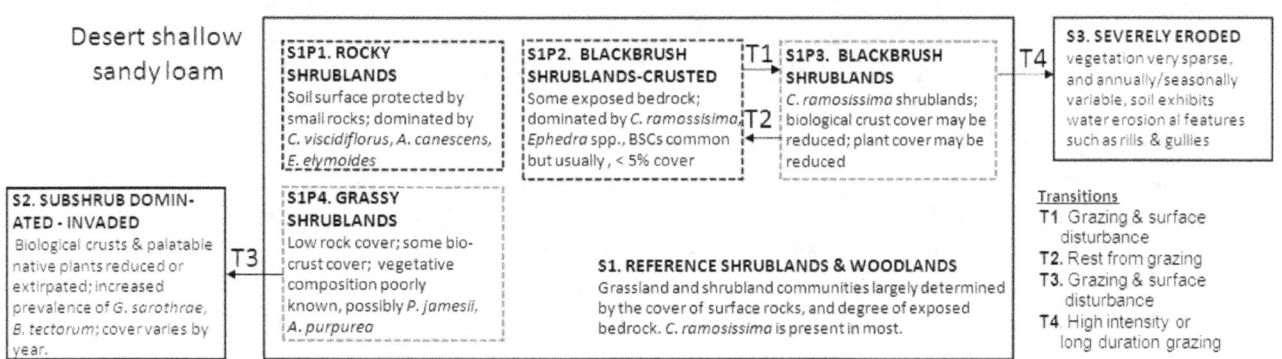

Figure 15. State-and-transition diagram for Desert shallow sandy loam. Boxes with solid outlinesrepresent ecosystem states. Boxes with dashed outlines indicate phases within states (red signifies a phase that is at-risk of transition to another state). Arrows indicate transitions. In some cases, phases within the reference state are not connected to any others by arrows; this is our method of representing spatial variants of the reference state that are dictated by abiotic factors.

S1. Reference shrublands and woodlands: Multiple distinct vegetative communities can be observed. They appear to largely be dictated by abiotic factors rather than disturbance and successional processes. Soil depth and proportion of the surface covered by rocks seem to determine dominant vegetation and biological soil crust cover (as rock increases, the amount of available habitat for crusts decreases). Most of the reference communities contain *C. ramosissima*. Sites with low to moderate surface rock and shallow depth (indicated by exposures of bedrock) tend to favor *C. ramosissima* shrublands.

S1 Phase1. Rocky shrublands. This phase is characterized by surfaces dominated by small rocks. The vegetative community is quite distinct, being dominated by *C. viscidiflorus*. *Elymus elymoides* and *A. canescens* are the most common palatable species. Biological soil crusts are not abundant, as there is little available habitat. Invasion by *Bromus tectorum* is uncommon, and of minor severity.

S1 Phase2. Blackbrush shrublands – crusted: This phase is characterized by low surface rock cover, and shallow soils indicated by bedrock exposures. The vegetation is naturally dominated by *C. ramosissima* and *Ephedra* spp. Biological soil crusts are often present, but cover generally is low. Invasion by *B. tectorum* is uncommon, and of minor severity.

S1 Phase3. Blackbrush shrublands: This phase is identical to S1P2 (Blackbrush shrublands - crusted), except that biological soil crust cover may be compromised by surface disturbances. Total plant cover may be reduced. Invasion by *B. tectorum* is uncommon, and of minor severity.

S1 Phase4. Grassy shrublands: This phase was not directly observed in available data, but is inferred based on a parallel phase in Semidesert shallow sandy loam sites. It is presumed to be the precursor of S2 (Annualized), although this cannot be tested directly since S2 sites occur only (with one exception) in currently grazed sites. Based on the native palatable species in S2, this phase might contain *Aristida purpurea* and *P. jamesii*. Biological soil crusts probably are common but not abundant.

S2. Subshrub dominated - invaded: Based on physical attributes (relatively low exposed bedrock and surface rock) and some floristic similarities, this state is likely to occur from grazing disturbance to S1P4 (Grassy shrublands). It is dominated by native unpalatable shrubs such as *G. sarothrae*. Additionally, *B. tectorum* may be a major community component, even codominating. Because of the potentially high contribution of *B. tectorum* to total cover, inter- and intraannual variation in total cover is possible. Biological soil crusts typically are eliminated or occur in low abundance.

S4. Severely eroded: This state is largely theoretical. When a site is naturally lacking in surface rocks, its soil erodibility can be enhanced by loss of biological soil crusts (this previously occurs in the transition from blackbrush shrublands-biological soil crusted to blackbrush shrublands). Erosivity, the ability of erosive forces to move sediment, is largely modified by properties of the plant community. Erodibility, the propensity for sediment to be moved by erosive forces, is largely determined by biological soil crusts on these sandy soils. When erodibility and erosivity are high, erosion is certain to occur. If grazing intensity or drought mortality (or other disturbance such as ORVs and seismic explorer rigs.) is so great that the erosivity-dampening properties of the vegetative community are degraded, a positive feedback may be initiated whereby erosion prevents vegetation recovery.

Transitions and Threshold Estimation

With the available data, we were able to model one transition for the Semidesert shallow sandy loam ecological site, transition 9 from grassy shrublands to the annualized state. The same model was not possible for the Desert shallow sandy loam ecological site, but we assume that the transition operates according to a similar mechanism.

Transition 9: S1P1 Grassy shrublands to S2 Subshrub dominated - invaded: Transition 9 was modeled according to a path model (fig. 16). Probability of state transition from grassy shrublands to subshrub dominated-invaded was predicted and simulated as a logistic function of relative cover of exotic species, biological soil crust cover, and total plant cover. Interrelationships among predictor variables were modeled as linear functions.
The equations were as follows

$$\text{log total plant cover} = 1.56 - 0.27 \text{ (grazing)} \tag{6}$$

$$\sqrt{\text{crust}} = 2.67 - 2.35 \text{ (grazing)} \tag{7}$$

$$
\begin{aligned}
\text{exotic annual rel. cover} = \quad & \tag{8} \\
5.93 + 0.30 & \text{ (grazing)} \\
- 4.10 & \text{ (log total plant cover)} \\
+ 0.05 & (\sqrt{\text{biological soil crust}}) \\
- 8.85 & \text{ (grazing} \times \text{log total plant cover)} \\
2.45 & (\sqrt{\text{biological soil crust}} \times \text{log total plant cover)} \\
+ 0.21 & (\sqrt{\text{biological soil crust}} \times \text{grazing)} \\
-5.93 & (\sqrt{\text{biological soil crust}} \times \text{grazing} \times \text{log total plant cover)}
\end{aligned}
$$

$$
\begin{aligned}
\text{probability of transition} = \quad & \tag{9} \\
1/1 +e -&(-0.0797 - 1.15(\text{log total plant cover}) - 1.96(\sqrt{\text{biological soil crust}}) + \\
& 2.69(\text{ exotic annual rel. cover)})
\end{aligned}
$$

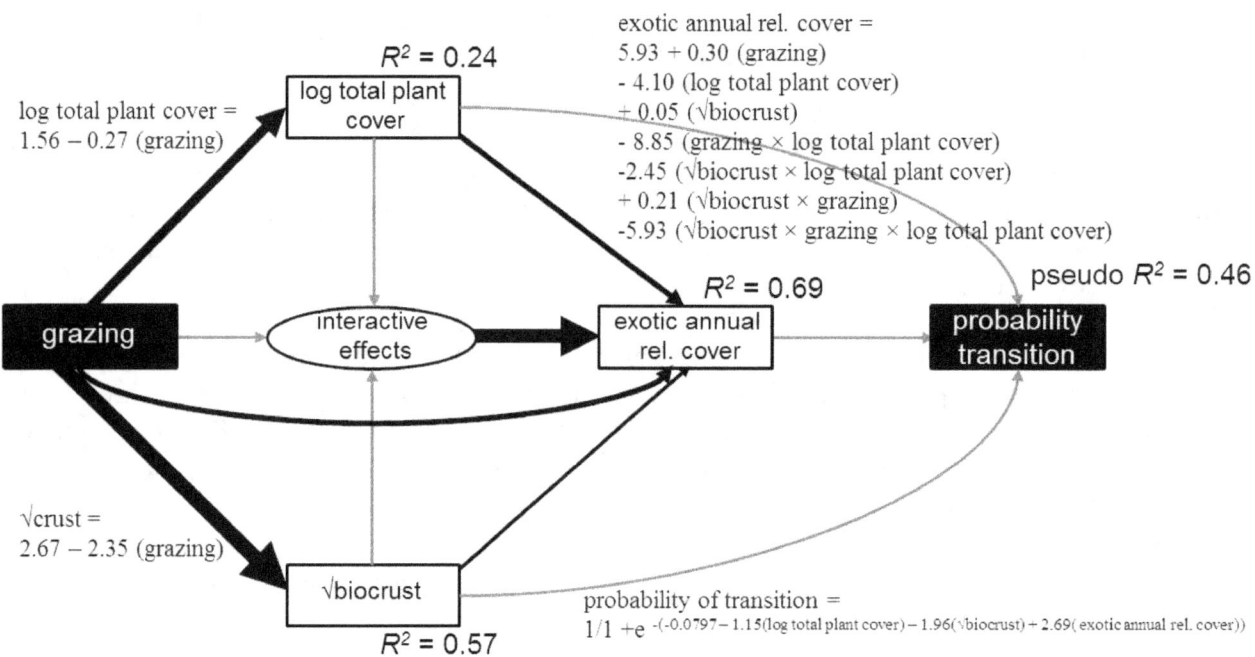

Figure 16. A path model showing the hypothesized mechanism underlying Transition 9. Boxes represent measured variables, dark filled boxes are binary data. Ovals represent interaction terms. Directed arrows are causal dependencies. Black arrows represent linear regression relationships, arrow width indicates the strength of the relationship. Gray arrows represent information flow from predictors in a logistic regression equation.

Simulations using this system of equations indicated that the greatest probabilities of transition observed were only about 50 percent. However, even if grazing is ceased there is still a small probability (about 5 percent) that transition will occur (fig. 17). This modeling exercise provides real values that can trigger management actions.

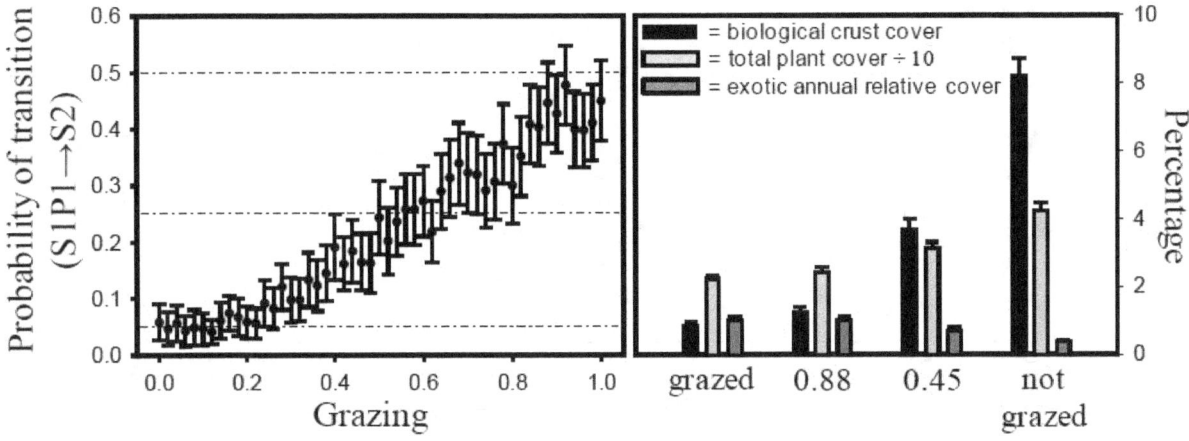

Figure 17. Modeled probabilities of transition from S1P4 to S2, given a range of grazing scenarios. Dashed lines represent critical probabilities (5 percent, 25 percent, and 50 percent). The right panels indicate values of monitored indicator variables corresponding to grazed and ungrazed scenarios, and transition probabilities of 25 percent and 50 percent.

Semidesert shallow sandy loam Transition 1 and 2: Wooded shrublands - crusted to Wooded shrublands (and reversed), Transition 3 and 4: Blackbrush shrublands - crusted to Blackbrush shrublands (and reversed) and Desert shallow sandy loam Transition 1 and 2: Blackbrush shrublands - crusted to Blackbrush shrublands (and reversed): These six transitions were considered together because they are within-state transitions among phases, they all involve a very similar dependency of soil stability on biological soil crust cover. They also are presumed to be reversible, if the stressor generating surface disturbance is removed. In both of the ecological sites, we hypothesize reference states with the potential to support a high cover of biological soil crusts, and the potential to transition to a severely eroded state is the biological soil crusts are lost. The severely eroded state was not directly observed. We hypothesized the existence of intermediate phases lying along these degradation sequences, woodlands, and shrublands lacking crusts, but otherwise similar to their crusted counterparts. This is because, in response to livestock grazing (the most common stressor), the condition of the soil surface is likely to be impacted faster than the predominantly woody, unpalatable vegetation, due to the inherent fragility of the soil surface. This phase transition is expected to increase erodibility, which may or may not lead to enhanced erosion. We hypothesize that under further pressure, the stature and spatial patterning of the woody vegetation changes in such a way that the ability of the vegetation to buffer erosivity of wind and water is reduced. When erodibility and erosivity are increased, a highly eroded state is possible.

Because these are not transitions among states, we were not expecting threshold-like behavior, rather we expected very strong linear dependencies. Nevertheless, we use the regression equations to estimate the biological soil crust cover at which soil stability was 5 percent, 25 percent, 50 percent, and 95 percent reduced to provide benchmarks for managing these ecosystems (fig. 18, table 3).

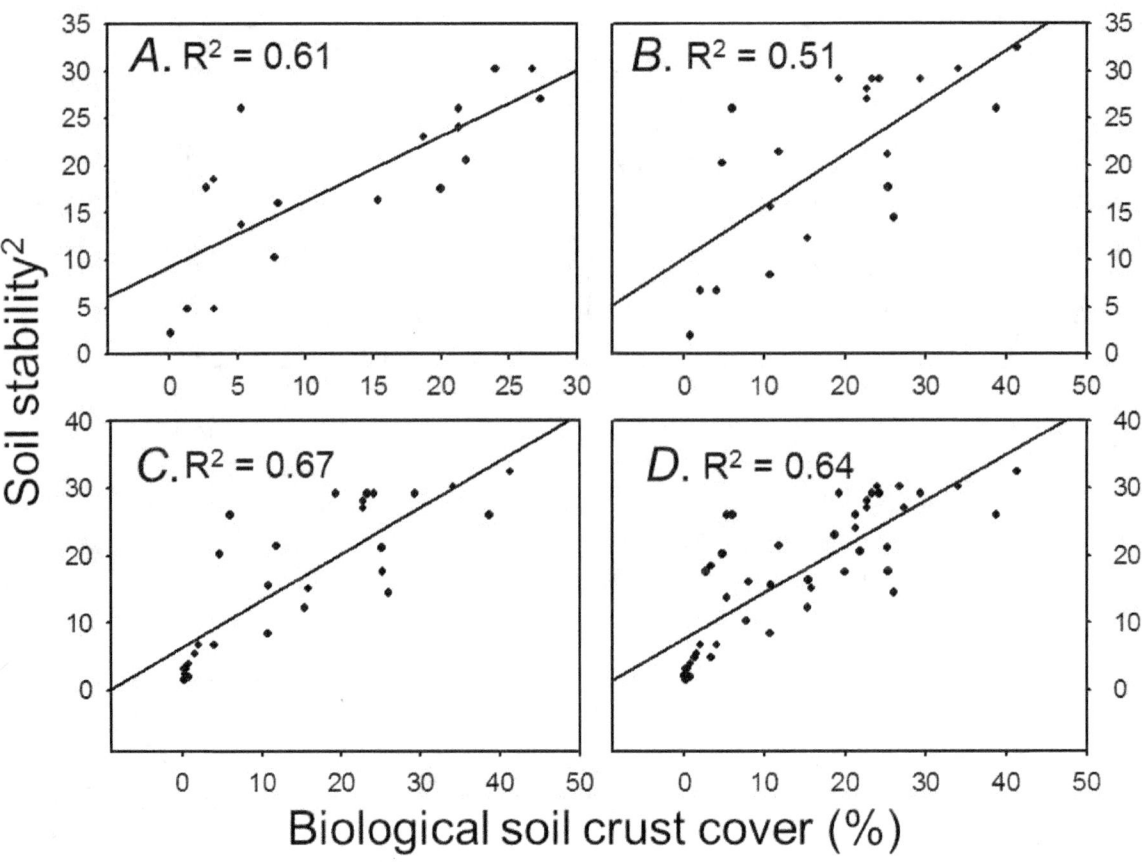

Figure 18. Linear regressions of soil stability as a function of biological soil crust cover in: *(A)* Wooded shrublands, *(B)* Semidesert blackbrush shrublands, *(C)* Desert and semidesert blackbrush shrublands, and *(D)* Pooled data.

Table 3. Biological soil crust cover at critical points in the degradation of soil stability. Percentages are based on a maximal value of 36, the square of the maximal value of the Herrick soil stability test (Herrick and others 2001).

Data	Degree of degradation of soil stability, in percentage			
	95 percent	50 percent	25 percent	5 percent
Semidesert wooded shrublands	0	12.6	25.5	35.9
Semidesert blackbrush shrublands	0	14.2	30.5	43.5
Desert and semidesert blackbrush shrublands	0	16.8	29.8	40.2
Pooled	0	15.1	28.3	38.9
Corresponding soil stability value	1.34	4.2	5.2	5.8

All regression equations, regardless of which input data were used, resulted in very similar values. Therefore the pooled regression may be the most useful because it pertains to all data. This regression suggests that to maintain the potential soil stability, biological soil crust cover (inclusive of moss, lichen, and cyanobacterial crust cover, and excluding physical crusts and soils with insufficient cyanobacterial density to aggregate soils) ought to be maintained at 38.9 percent.

Interpretation

In the case of these two ecological sites, Semidesert shallow sandy loam and Desert shallow sandy loam, the reference state was very broadly defined with spatial variants. The original ecological site description does not seem to adequately capture the variation in vegetation community structure. The description also greatly underestimates the potential abundance of biological soil crusts. We suggest that two states exist outside of the reference state, an annualized state and a severely eroded state. We detected a wide range of biological soil crust cover in wooded shrublands and blackbrush shrublands that did not support the designation of separate biological soil crusted and uncrusted states; instead, these were maintained as phases within the refence state. This is common to both ecological sites, but in both cases, the severely eroded state is only hypothesized, not observed. A phase with a considerable grass component is observed in semidesert shallow sandy loam; here we make an assumption that, although it was not sampled, it also exists in desert shallow sandy loam. Alternatively, this ecological site may be too dry to support this phase. Not all aspects of the state-and-transition models presented here have been validated with data and thus remain hypothetical.

When considering data from grassy shrubland and subshrub-dominated clusters, our analyses indicate that even in a currently ungrazed state there is still a small but reasonable chance that annualization has occurred. We may interpret this as being due to past grazing-induced transitions that persisted after grazing ceased, or that despite low grazing disturbance, invasion may occur anyway perhaps aided by climate change. When relative exotic annual cover reaches about 1 percent, and/or when two of its causal influences (crust cover and total plant cover), are reduced to 3.7 and 31.4 percent, respectively, an assessment of the necessity of management actions (for example, modifications of grazing regime) may occur. These are the points at which transition to an annualized state become 25 percent probable. When relative exotic annual cover reaches about 1.0, crusts are reduced to 1.2 percent and total plant cover is reduced to 24.3 percent, a management action is needed (for example, cessation of grazing or active restoration). If a management response is not undertaken, a transition will become as likely as not. This transition represents a management dilemma, in that the grassy shrublands probably represent the best forage producing state in the ecological site, but utilizing the forage comes with a risk of inducing annualization of this particularly susceptible phase.

Although we lacked the data to test the assumption, we suspect that a similar mechanism underlies the corresponding Transition 3 in the ecological site desert shallow sandy loam, and that a similar management recommendation can be made regarding this site.

If we consider the transition to the severely eroded state, we have no direct observations of the end member. However, we can model the process that we hypothesize to be involved, which is the loss of erosion resistance as a function of diminishing biological soil crust cover in certain phases of the reference state. Degradation of biological soil crusts and resistance to erosion are characteristics of phases at-risk of transition to a severely eroded state. It is not known to what degree erosion resistance can be degraded before such a transition is probable. If our model is correct, simply not allowing surface disturbance that diminished biological soil crusts would be sufficient to safeguard against this transition.

If land is being managed for uses which require surface disturbance, soil stability can be maintained at 75 percent of its potential, if crust cover is maintained at at least 28.3 percent. Likewise, soil stability can be maintained at 50 percent of its potential, if at least 15.1 percent crust cover is retained. Beyond this point, a site is increasingly likely to have passed into an at-risk phase. The at-risk phases, if further damaged, are susceptible to transition to severely eroded states. These values pertain to both ecological sites considered here.

Climate Change-Driven Transitions

The two ecological sites are very closely aligned and can be viewed simply as a wetter and drier version of the same ecological setting with much overlap in form and function. Recent global-change type droughts in the Colorado Plateau region suggest that drought mortality can occur quickly in pulses (Breshears and others, 2005; Gitlin and others, 2006; Allen and others, 2010). *P. edulis* is particularly susceptible. We can consider that a prolonged drying trend or an extreme drought could change the states and phases presented for semidesert shallow sandy loam to corresponding states and phases in desert shallow sandy loam. Another state-and-transition model can illustrate possible transitions between these two ecological sites (fig. 19).

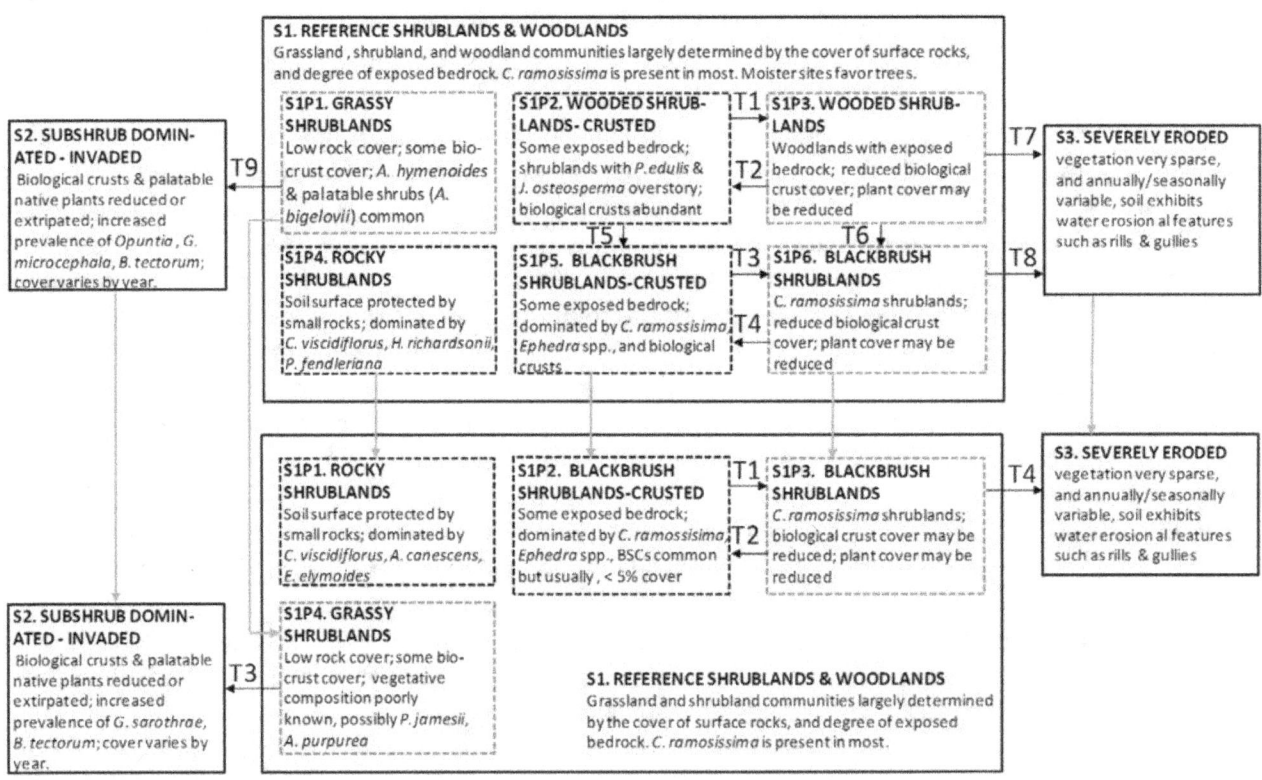

Figure 19. State and transition model linking states and phases in Semidesert shallow sandy loam and Desert shallow sandy loam because of drought-linked transitions.

Case Study 5: Semidesert Stony Loam (Shadscale)

Introduction

Semidesert stony loam (Shadscale) ecological sites, are situated on stony, often cobbly alluvial and colluvial soils. They are deep and well drained, and typically occur on mild to moderate slopes. They are at least slightly calcareous, ranging up to about 30 percent $CaCO_3$. A large proportion of the soil surface is covered by rock, making the soil well-armored against wind erosion, but these soils may be susceptible to water erosion, especially on steeper slopes.

The current draft ecological site description (ftp://ftp-fc.sc.egov.usda.gov/UT/Range/D35XY/035XY242UT.pdf) does not provide a state-and-transition model, but does mention some vegetation characteristics and some ecosystem dynamics in response to grazing and fire. According to the description, potential dominant vegetation is dominated by *Atriplex confertifolia* and *Pleuraphis jamesii*, and contains perennial grasses and shrubs in roughly equal proportions. *Achnatherum hymenoides* is a subdominant grass, and *Ephedra torreyana*, *Artemisia bigelovii*, and *Krascheninikovia lanata* are subdominant shrubs. The Soil Conservation Service often described grazing increasers and decreasers in range site descriptions, specific to a given range site. The NRCS continues to do so in ecological site descriptions. Decreasers tend to decrease under grazing pressure because they are intolerant to grazing pressure, or are preferentially consumed due to palatability. Increasers tend to increase under grazing pressure because they are tolerant of grazing pressure, unpalatable, or experience competitive release with grazing. Under grazing, decreasers include *Hesperostipa comata*, *A. hymenoides*, *A. bigelovii*, and *E. torreyana* (all palatable except for *Ephedra*). Grazing increasers include *Artemisia tridentata*, *Gutierrezia sarothrae*, *P. jamesii*, and *A. confertifolia* (*Pleuraphis* and *Atriplex* are palatable). Biological soil crust cover of only 1 percent is mentioned in the description. *Bromus tectorum*, *Pinus edulis*, *Juniperus osteosperma*, and *Helianthus anuum* are listed as possible "invaders", although all of these are native except for *B. tectorum*.

Methods Details

A Priori Model of Ecosystem Dynamics

We adopted a two-state model based on the hypothesized grazing impacts stated above. We conceived of a referenced state with one phase dominated by the grazing decreasers and another dominated by the grazing increasers. We hypothesized that these phases might not clearly separate, because transitions back and forth are relatively easy and contingent on site grazing history. We also hypothesized a severely eroded state wherein erosion processes prevent recolonization of plants.

Although fire dynamics are mentioned in the ecological site description, our *a priori* state and transition model did not include fire-related transitions because these communities are characterized by low cover and are inherently resistant to burning and carrying fire. We also did not consider the tree invasion scenarios proposed in the ecological site description because these xeric sites have poor water holding capacity not favoring trees; furthermore, trees have been particularly susceptible to recent droughts suggesting that they are not likely to be captured invading in recent data (Breshears and others, 2005; Gitlin and others, 2006; Bowker and others, 2012b). However, NCPN staff have observed this dynamic on nearby very steep stony loam sites. We did not rule out the possibility of *Helianthus* becoming a community component, but did not hypothesize a state or phase dominated by this species. NCPN staff have not observed this phase in the field.

Data

We analyzed a total of 29 samples; 15 samples originated from 3 sources in the NCPN database, primarily in and around Capitol Reef National Park. Of these, four were from the Grand Staircase-Escalante National Monument Rangeland Health dataset (Miller 2008), another eight were supplied by the NPS I&M plots of Capitol Reef National Park (Witwicki 2009b), and three were originally sourced from the Capitol Reef Vegetation Map Dataset (Clark and others, 2009). Shane Green of the NRCS provided some vegetative composition data from an additional 14 sites that were on file compiled by unidentified authors (S. Green, Natural Resource Conservation Service, written comm., 2011); the location of these was not documented in the data files. The data used described relative abundance of plants by species.

Cluster Analysis

We subjected all available data on plant community composition to hierarchical cluster analysis in PC-ORD™ (MJM Software Design, Gleneden Beach, Oregon) to determine if clusters could validate the existence of *a priori* states and phases. All species with fewer than three occurrences were excluded from the analysis. We applied a relativization-by-row maximum transformation to focus the analysis on relative species abundance. A double relativization to further standardize data was not appropriate, because the NRCS data did not provide absolute abundance of species, only relative abundance. Based on a rather simple *a priori* concept of a state with two phases (one dominated by grazing decreasers and one dominated by grazing increasers), and an additional devegetated state subject to erosion, we examined two-, three- and four-cluster solutions. We selected an appropriate number of clusters based on information remaining in the cluster diagram and on subjective interpretability.

As an interpretational aid we also ordinated our data using non-metric multidimensional scaling (NMDS). To visualize the differences among clusters in ordination space we rescaled symbols based on the relative abundance of particular species. We used these results as a basis to develop our final state-and-transition model. Clusters generally correspond to states or phases in the model.

Modeling Transitions

After developing a final state-and-transition model, we modeled all five transitions proposed in the model. We found that a complex model was not required to provide a mechanistic model of transition among these states and phases, based on the small amount of data we had available. Rather, univariate logistic regression models were used based on functionally significant predictors that were available in the dataset. We parameterized the regression equation and solved for all possible values of the predictor variable being used. This enabled us to view a smooth, continuous surface to find key breakpoints in the probability of cluster membership: 5 percent, 25 percent, 50 percent, and 95 percent percent. Because clusters approximate our concept of states or phases, we interpreted these probabilities as probabilities of transition from one state to another.

Results

Cluster Analysis

We selected a four-cluster solution as the best grouping of available data. These were all "clean" clusters with little overlap and all could be potentially explained by a hypothetical unquantified grazing gradient (from lower right to upper left in each panel of fig. 20). Based on the four-cluster solution, we determined the degree of correlation of various species with the clusters. We found that there were clusters indicated by: (*A*) *A. canescens*, (*B*) *A. confertifolia*, and (*C*) *P. jamesii* and (*D*) *B. tectorum* (fig. 20).

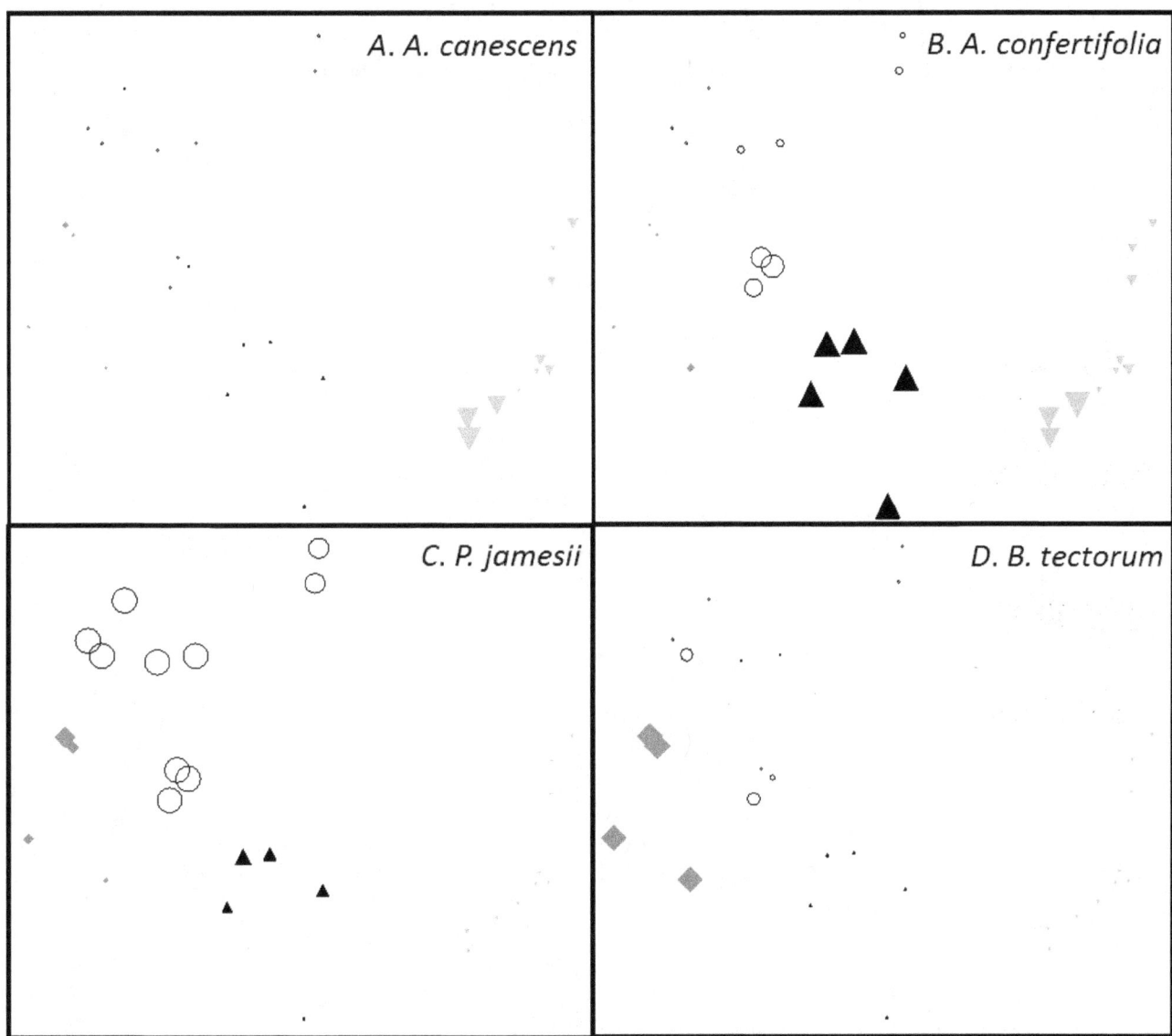

Figure 20. Diagram showing same ordination with symbols resized to reflect the relative abundance of key species. (*A*) Symbols resized relative to the abundance of *A. canescens*. (*B*) Symbols resized relative to the abundance of *A. confertifolia*. (*C*) Symbols resized relative to the abundance of *P. jamesii*. (*D*) Symbols resized relative to the abundance of *B. tectorum*.

Final State-and-Transition Model

The clusters depicted in panels *A–C* seem to correspond well to NRCS concepts of vegetation changes under grazing pressure (loss of decreasers, expansion of increasers). All three of these could be interpreted as different phases of the same state; because of the shift in growth form dominance, we interpreted a perennial grass-rich cluster (open circles) as its own state. There also was an unexpected detection of a *B. tectorum*-dominated cluster (closed diamonds), which we deemed functionally distinct enough to be its own state. We hypothesized that this *B. tectorum*-dominated state can emerge from the *P. jamesii*-dominated cluster (open circles) because: (1) the latter are the closest cluster in ordination space, and (2) the grazing is commonly thought to enhance *B. tectorum* invasion, In evidence of the latter, the *P. jamesii* cluster is more dominated by grazing increasers, and the *P. jamesii* cluster is probably more strongly grazing impacted and more susceptible to invasion. We cannot rule out that this state emerged from a cluster other than the *P. jamesii*-dominated cluster.

With these results in mind we developed the following state-and-transition model (fig. 21).

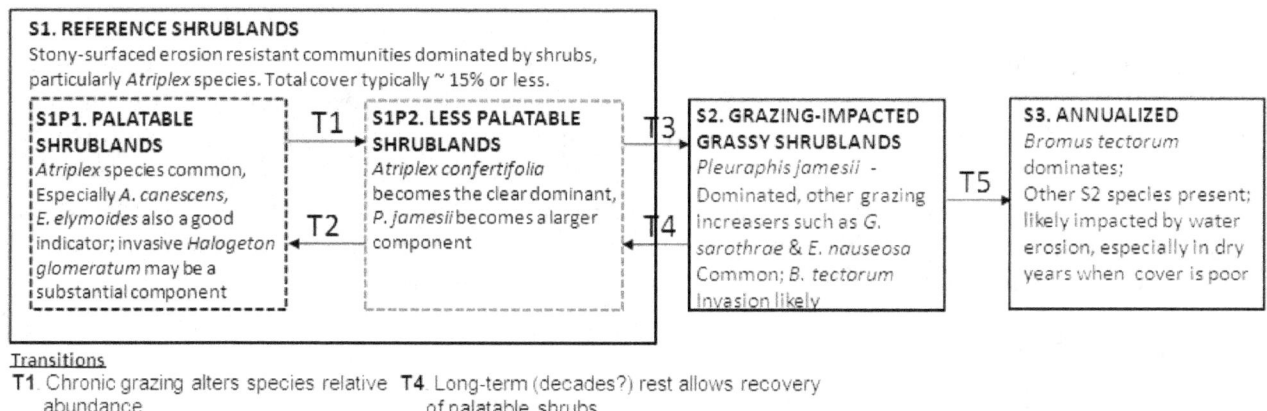

Figure 21. State-and-transition diagram for semidesert stony loam (shadscale). Solid boxes refer to ecosystem states, and dashed boxes represent phases within those states (red being at-risk of state transition).

S1. Reference shrublands: State one consists of sparse shrublands over shallow soils with a large amount of surface rock. *A. confertifolia* is a common species, which may co-occur with *Atriplex canescens*, *Artemisia* spp., and *E. torreyana*. There may be a grass component such as *H. comata*, *A. hymenoides*, *P. jamesii,* or *Elymus elymoides*. Rock cover is 35 percent on average, ranging from 9 to 75 percent. Biological soil crusts may be present but habitat is constrained by rock cover. Plant cover averages 18 percent, with most sites having less cover and some extremely productive sites with cover up to 45 percent. Shrubs are usually about twice as abundant as grasses. A large proportion of the soil is armored by rock but soil aggregate stability of exposed soil surface may be low, averaging 2–3 using the Herrick soil stability kit (Herrick and others, 2001). As in many ecological sites, surface soil stability is controlled largely by biological soil crust cover, which explain around 60 percent of the variation in aggregate stability.

S1 Phase1. Palatable shrublands: Total plant cover is about 15 percent, and a typical shrub to grass ratio is about 5:1. These sites are more likely to contain cool season bunchgrasses, such as *A. hymenoides* and *H. comata*, the palatable shrubs *A. bigelovii* and *A. canescens*, and the unpalatable *E. torreyana*. Biological soil crust cover is usually sparse.

S1 Phase2. Less palatable shrublands: Total plant cover is about 8 percent, and a typical shrub to grass ratio is about 3.3:1. These sites are most likely to contain higher relative abundance of *A. confertifolia*, along with unpalatable shrubs *G. sarothrae*. The warm season perrennial grass *P. jamesii* may increase in importance. Biological soil crust cover is usually sparse. *J. osteosperma* may occasionally be an important species.

S2. Grazing-impacted grassy shrubland: Total plant cover is about 28 percent, though smaller statured species are dominant, suggesting that standing biomass may be lower than the previous state. A typical shrub to grass ratio is about 1. This state is dominated by the grazing tolerant grass, *P. jamesii*, and the palatable shrubs are greatly reduced. *G. sarothrae* is a common subdominant and *B. tectorum* may have invaded.

S3. Annualized: Information on total plant cover is lacking, because samples documenting this state are associated only with relative cover data. Palatable shrubs have largely been replaced by unpalatable shrubs such as *C. ramosissima* and *G. sarothrae*. Grasses typically account for more cover than shrubs by a ratio of about 3.5:1. This is driven by annual grasses which account for about 70 percent of the grass cover; the perrennial grass to shrub ratio is close to 1. *B. tectorum* dominates, and as a result, vegetative cover fluctuates within and among years. The exposed soil surface is erodible, especially in highly erosive thunderstorms, but there is little exposed soil surface because of rock cover.

Transitions and Threshold Estimation

We considered all five transitions proposed in our state-and-transition model for semidesert stony loam using logistic regression (fig. 22). Transitions 1 and 2 follow an identical model based on the ratio of grazing decreaser plants to increaser plants (summed cover) as defined by the NRCS ecological site description (ftp://ftp-fc.sc.egov.usda.gov/UT/Range/D35XY/035XY242UT.pdf). Transition 2 is simply a reversal of transition 1. Likewise, transitions 3 and 4 follow the same model based on the ratio of the summed cover of perennial grasses to the summed cover of shrubs. Transition 4 is simply a reversal of transition 3. Transition 5 was based on the summed cover of exotic annuals.

Transition 1 (and)2. S1P1 Palatable shrublands to S1P2 Less palatable shrublands (and vice-versa)
Transition 1 can be modeled by the logistic function, with a pseudo R^2 of 0.56.

$$\text{probability of transition} = \frac{1}{1 + e^{-(1.6089 - 8.9706(\text{decreasers/increasers}))}} \tag{10}$$

Transition 2 can be modeled by using the negatives of the slope and intercept parameters of equation 10.

$$\text{probability of transition} = \frac{1}{1 + e^{-(-1.6089 + 8.9706(\text{decreasers/increasers}))}} \tag{11}$$

Transition 3 (and 4): S1P2 Less palatable shrublands to S2 Grazing-impacted grassy shrublands (and vice-versa)
Transition 3 can be modeled by the logistic function, with a pseudo R^2 of 0.82.

$$\text{probability of transition} = \frac{1}{1 + e^{-(15.86395 - 31.3721(\text{grass/shrub}))}} \tag{12}$$

Transition 4 can be modeled by using the negatives of the slope and intercept parameters of equation 12.

$$\text{probability of transition} = \frac{1}{1 + e^{-(-15.86395 + 31.3721(\text{grass/shrub}))}} \tag{13}$$

Transition 5. S2 Grazing-impacted grassy shrublands to S3 Annualized: Transition 5 can be modeled by the following logistic function. This function based on the available data was "perfect" in the sense that the two groups of data (S2 and S3) did not overlap, leading to a pseudo R^2 of 1.0. Thus, multiple parameters are possible solutions and the solution provided here is unstable. In practice, this is not important because the boundary between the two states is in the narrow range between 27 and 28 percent exotic annual cover.

$$\text{probability of transition} = \tag{14}$$
$$1/1 + e - (198.2512 - 720.8806(\text{exotic annual cover}))$$

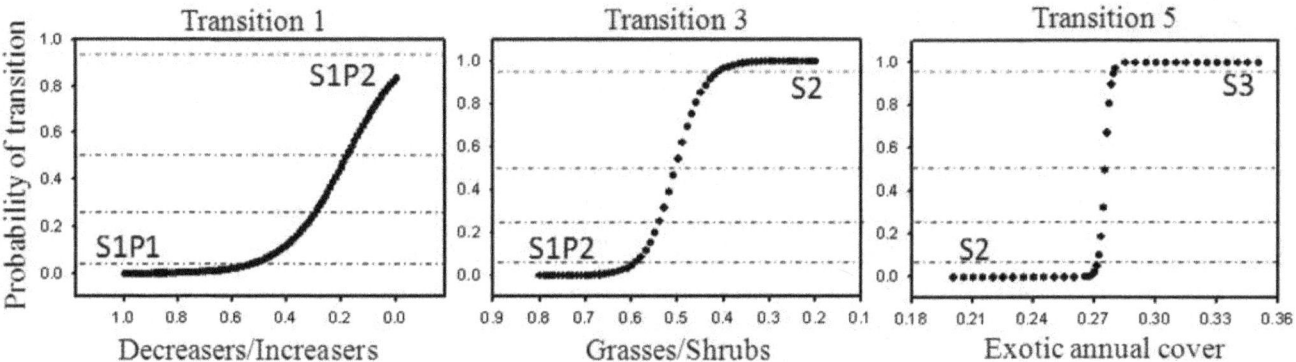

Figure 22. Logistic equations of transitions 1,3, and 5, predicting the probability of transition. Dashed horizontal lines depict critical probabilities (5 percent, 25 percent, 50 percent, and 95 percent).

This modeling exercise provides real values which can trigger management actions. The values corresponding to all five transitions are shown in table 4.

Table 4. Critical probabilities of transition given values of monitorable predictors for five transitions.

Transition	Predictor	Probability (percent)	Value
T1: S1P1→S1P2	Decreasers/increasers	5 percent	0.51
		25 percent	0.3
		50 percent	0.18
T2: S1P2→S1P1	Decreasers/increasers	25 percent	0.06
		50 percent	0.18
		95 percent	0.51
T3: S1P2→S2	Grasses/Shrubs	5 percent	0.41
		25 percent	0.47
		50 percent	0.51
		95 percent	0.6
T4: S2→S1P2	Grasses/Shrubs	5 percent	0.6
		25 percent	0.54
		50 percent	0.51
		95 percent	0.41
T5: S2→S3	Exotic annual cover	5 percent	0.271
		25 percent	0.275
		50 percent	0.277
		95 percent	0.279

Interpretation

Unlike many semi-arid ecosystems, grazing pressure in semidesert stony loam (shadscale) primarily takes the form of shifts in vegetation composition and do not degrade soil surfaces. All transitions are assumed to be driven at least partially by grazing pressure. If Decreasers/Increasers defined by NRCS are used as an index of the grazing pressure on community composition, a negligible probability (less than 5 percent) of transition from S1P1 (palatable shrublands) to S1P2 (less palatable shrublands) exists if decreasers compose 51 percent or more of the community. If grazing is allowed to decrease this ratio to 30 percent, a transition would not be an uncommon event (25 percent probability), and if the ratio decreases to 18 percent, transition is just as probable as no transition (50 percent probability). If these probabilities of transition are too high given management priorities, relaxation of grazing might be prescribed. Using this predictor, near certainty (95 percent transition probability) of transition is not observed even if all decreasers are eliminated. This implies that there is another unmeasured driver of transition that is not incorporated into the model.

If transition does occur to S1 Phase2 (less palatable shrublands), the ecosystem is then at-risk for transition to a new state with an increase in prevalence of grazing tolerant grasses (state 2). Whether or not this constitutes degradation depends on management goals. Again, grazing pressure is assumed to underly this transition. Grasses may compose as much as 41 percent of the community without a transition being probable (5 percent probability). However, if grasses (primarily *P. jamesii*) are allowed to increase to 51 percent, a transition is about as probable as not (50 percent probability). Transition becomes nearly certain because grasses compose 60 percent of the community. Again, if these probabilities of transition are too high given management priorities, relaxation of grazing might be prescribed.

Although state 2 (grazing-impacted grassy shrublands) may still retain considerable forage for grazing, the primary management concern with state 2 is that it may be susceptible to annualization. We do not know with certainty that state 3 does emerge from state 2; other scenarios are plausible. In any case, the key variables to monitor will be the more direct descriptors of annualization. The best measure of annualization would be the intra- and interannual variation in vegetation cover. We did not have this data to work with, thus we used exotic annual cover as our predictor. Regardless of land use preferences, annualization by exotics is never desired. Our data indicate a very sharp boundary between grazing-impacted grassy shrublands and annualized states. For less than 27 percent exotic annual cover, transition is highly improbable. For greater than 28 percent exotic annual cover, transition is nearly certain. Thus, if 27 percent exotic annual cover is close to being attained, management intervention should occur to increase perennial species or reduce exotic annuals.

Caveats and Alternative Explanations

Our observed clusters generally seem to provide a reasonable validation of the NRCS ecological site description. We perceive a gradient of communities, dominated by putative decreaser species identified in the description, grade into communities dominated by increaser species, which in turn grades into states dominated by exotic invasive grasses. To our knowledge, all our sites are currently in active grazing allotments and have likely been affected by livestock in recent years; from these results we would infer that the more strongly affected cluster had experienced more grazing activity.

Our designations of clusters into three distinct states rests on two key changes in plant growth form or phenological dominance. First, a transition from strong dominance by shrubs to a relatively equal representation of shrubs and grasses occurs (S1. Reference shrublands to S2. Grazing-impacted grassy shrublands). Second, a transition from strong dominance by perennials to co-dominance by annuals occurs (S2. Grazing-impacted grassy shrublands to S3. Annualized). Based on typical invasion scenarios, the second transition probably is persistent, however, it is not known how persistent the first transition is. State-and-transition models are always inherently partly subjective and the data and observations used to verify them are often incomplete. An alternative model might consider S2 to be a phase of S1 that could revert passively back to shrub dominance.

We cannot rule out observer bias in generating these differences in this data-poor ecological site. The annualized cluster is exclusively derived from data provided by the NRCS. The less impacted cluster are primarily sites sampled by the NPS I&M program, whereas the other cluster consists of a mixture of sites from the Capitol Reef National Park vegetation mapping project and from the Grand Staircase-Escalante National Monument Rangeland Health Assessment. Biases could be present resulting from different personnel collecting data, or the more southerly distribution of the samples in the more impacted cluster.

Case Study 6: Clayey Fans

Background

The NRCS has prepared an ecological site description for Clayey fans (*https://esis.sc.egov.usda.gov/ESDReport/fsReport.aspx?approved=yes&id=R035XB239AZ*) but it currently lacks an STM. Clayey Fans are fluvio-alluvial features below the exposures of the Chinle Formation in the painted desert region, including Petrified Forest National Park. Soils are loamy, ranging from fine sandy loams to clay loams and sandy clay loams. The proportion of clay probably represents the influence of the Chinle Formation relative to other coarser parent materials. The soils are of shallow to moderate depth. Precipitation ranges from 15 to 25 cm/yr (610 in/yr) in the form of cool season rain and snow, and high intensity summer monsoons. Elevations are around 1,800 m (5,500 ft). Currently vegetation is primarily grasslands variously dominated by *Sporobolus airoides*, or *Pleuraphis jamesii*, with a shrub component most often composed of *Atriplex obovata* or *Atriplex canescens*. The ecological site description states that *Salsola* spp. and *Bromus tectorum* are often present and could severely invade under disturbance. Another invasive with potential to invade is *Alhagi marourum*. The descriptions suggest that *Ericameria nauseosa, Gutierrezia sarothrae*, cacti, and annuals are the most likely to increase in abundance with grazing. The current description does not specifically mention decreasers but does suggest that unpalatable shrub dominance is more likely to emerge under grazing, implying that the major grasses and palatable shrubs are decreasers. An early range site description suggested the possibility of a *Juniperus* invasion (Miller, 1975), although this dynamic is not mentioned in later descriptions.

Methods Details

A Priori State and Transition Models

Based on the ecological site description, we hypothesized a simple three-state model containing a grass-dominated reference state with a shrub component, an annualized state dominated by *Bromus* or more likely, *Salsola*, and because of the inherently low soil stability, a severely eroded state. The prospect of a *Juniperus* invasion of more than a few isolated individuals seemed implausible, so it was not considered.

Data

There is considerable data on the vegetation community composition in 128 vegetation surveys in a recent USGS vegetation mapping effort (Thomas and others, 2009). The detailed data contain only one case (plot-level datapoint) where grazing, the most likely stressor, is active. Otherwise grazing has been retired within the park for more than 40 years, making this dataset unlikely to reveal the outcome of heavy grazing. Data on ecosystem functional attributes, ground cover, or spatial attributes of vegetation are confined to only 10 datapoints in DeCoster and Swan (2009a), and to another 10 added later. Thus, data on the range of community structure are fairly rich, but data on ecosystem function are sparse. This will change as the NPS I&M program expands its monitoring network, and analysis of transitions and thresholds may become possible.

Analysis of Grazing Impacts and Rebound from Grazing

Rebound from grazing and vegetational successional dynamics were analyzed in two ways: (1) using a dataset describing the first 20 years of vegetation change on two transects (G Johnson, National Park Service, unpub. data, 1984) and (2) using a space-for-time replacement analysis based on a vegetative mapping dataset collected from 2003 to 2006, and exploiting a south to north gradient in completion of the park boundary fence from 1934 to 1963.

Temporal transect data: George Johnson, a ranger at Petrified Forest, initiated a range recovery study in 1972, on two transects representing Clayey fans. The transects were within 100 m of one another and represented a former corral and watering area for cattle (G Johnson, National Park Service, unpub. data, 1984). Johnson sampled vegetation in 1972, 1974, 1976, 1978, 1982, and 1984. Peter Rowlands relocated and sampled the transects in 1992. No one has resampled the transects after the drought years of 1996 and 2002–03.

Rowlands (P. Rowlands, unpub. data, 1992) identified several interpretational problems. Principal among them were: (1) the transects are in atypical low-lying areas that have higher than typical potential for vegetative cover; (2) Johnson sampled in early spring in 1972 and 1974, but shifted to the summer monsoon season afterward; (3) the initial years of the study also coincided with increasing precipitation, making it difficult to separate dynamics driven by succession, and those driven solely by precipitation; and (4) Johnson used a small number of points for a point intercept method. Nevertheless, these data represent the only quantitative document of temporal change in vegetation on Clayey fans.

In this report we replot all available data from the transects. Additionally, we examined the spatial patterns in this spatially explicit data for the first time. Taking note of the identity and the location of each point intercept we plotted the transect data through time.

Vegetation map data: Petrified Forest National Park consists of northern and southern blocks connected by a narrow strip of park lands. Fencing and phasing out of grazing was conducted gradually, starting in the south in the mid 1930s. The north boundary fence was not completed until 1963. The distribution of Clayey fans within the park also is bimodal with a northern cluster and a southern cluster. Therefore, differences in the vegetation monitoring dataset (Thomas and others 2009) between the northern and southern clusters in terms of vegetation composition and cover might reflect different lengths of time since boundary fencing was completed, and grazing was excluded. We cannot rule out that any differences are because of other factors that differ among the northern and southern clusters.

We coded each Clayey fan sample as belonging to the northern or southern block and created an NMDS ordination of the data. We account for which species cause any separation among groups in two ways: (1) rotating the ordination so that axis 1 maximizes the difference between northern and southern clusters, and then obtaining the correlations of each species with axis 1, and (2) conducting an indicator species analysis. We also conducted t-tests comparing total cover and plant diversity among northern and southern blocks.

Cluster Analysis

We validated and revised our *a priori* state-and-transition models by conducting a hierarchical cluster analysis of vegetation community composition from the vegetation map dataset (Thomas and others, 2009). We applied a relativization by species transformation, equalizing the influence of each column. Based on the expected number of clusters in our *a priori* models (3), we examined results for two- to eight-cluster solutions. Cluster analyses are subjective descriptive tools and should not be viewed as strict hypothesis tests. We used the following guidelines to select the best number of clusters: (1) Acknowledging that we may not observe all states in our *a priori* model (and that their absence does not prove they do not exist) and that additional clusters may exist that we did not anticipate, we selected a solution with a number of clusters reasonably small; (2) we accepted clusters that were a good match with our *a priori* expectations, if they existed; (3) we accepted unanticipated clusters when they were consistent with a mechanistic explanation as to how they could emerge (for example, determined by abiotic factors, or a likely outcome of a given disturbance). We selected the solution that *best* satisfied *all* of the above criteria. To help us define the characteristics of our clusters, we applied indicator species analysis (Dufrene and Legendre, 1997), and viewed NMDS ordinations. We updated our state-and-transition concept based on the results of the cluster analysis.

Modeling Transitions

We examined the DeCoster and Swan (2009a) dataset, but based on our cluster analyses and resultant STM (fig. 28) we found little evidence that this dataset had captured any departures from the reference state. The number of samples in Thomas and others (2009) was large, but the number of samples that may have transitioned outside of the reference state was small. We investigated transition 6 for which we had 25 relevant samples. We had some difficulty finding covergent models with multiple predictors. Therefore, we used a simple univariate logistic regression using total plant cover as a predictor.

Results

Temporal Transect Data

Total cover increases impressively (almost an order of magnitude on transect B1) and nearly linearly over this time span (fig. 23). Rowlands cautioned that the increase in Johnson's data may be due to annually increasing precipitation during this time (P. Rowlands, National Park Service, unpub. data, 1992) However, the vegetation continued increasing at a similar rate through the late 1980s and early 1990s, when this precipitation trend did not hold, suggesting that a simple "time since fencing" model is the most parsimonious predictor of this change.

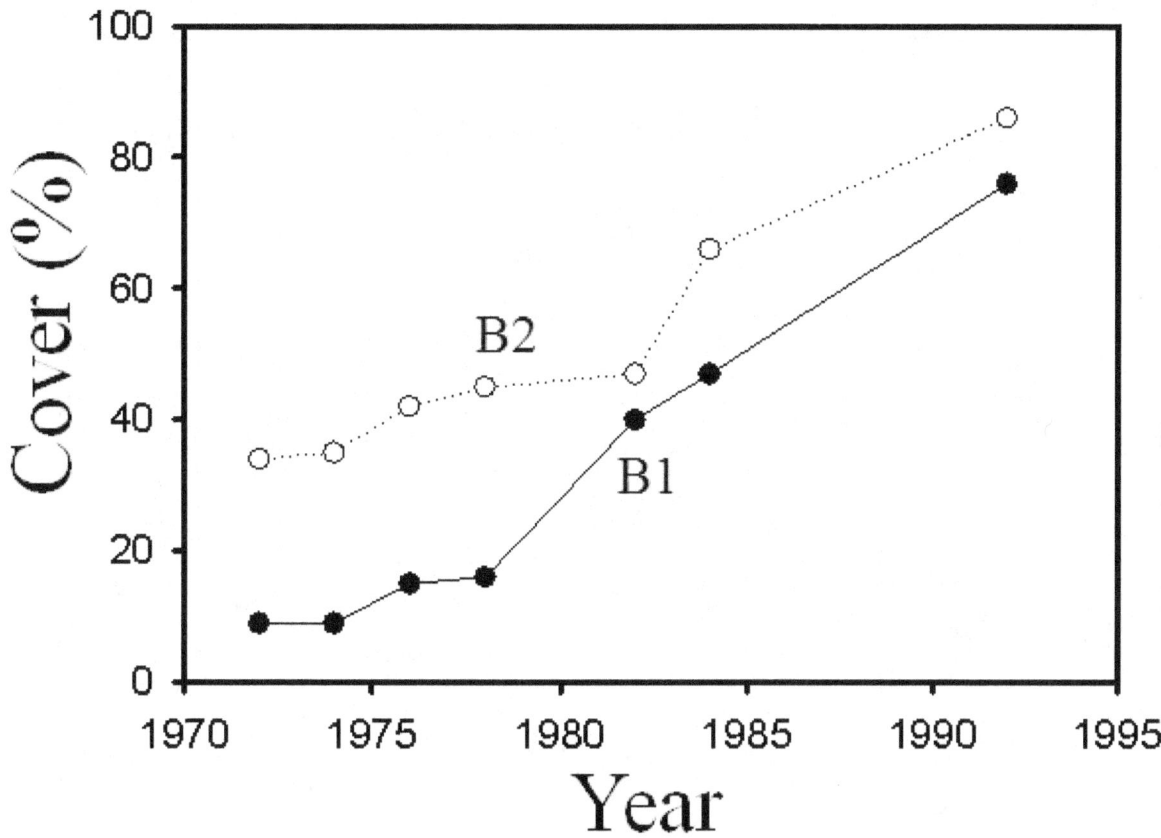

Figure 23. Graph showing increase in vegetation over time after the cessation of grazing on two transects on Clayey Fans.

Vegetation change did not conform to the model expressed in the ecological site description. Under intense grazing pressure, we would have expected a major decline in *S. airoides* and replacement with annuals, cacti, *E. nauseosum,* and *G. sarothrae*. The latter three were never observed. The 1972 communities were *S. airoides*-dominated, and remained so throughout the monitoring period. There was a clear spatial dependency from one year to the next, where new colonization events strongly tended to be in a previously occupied position on the transect or adjacent (fig. 24). Most of the occupied portions on the transects can be traced backward to a position previously occupied by *S. aroides*, or a position adjacent. This suggests *S. airoides* as a grazing-resilient facilitator of community recovery. Transect B1 seemed to add species over time, with multiple shrubs becoming more important, especially *Atriplex* spp. In contrast, transect B2 had most of its species present from very early on.

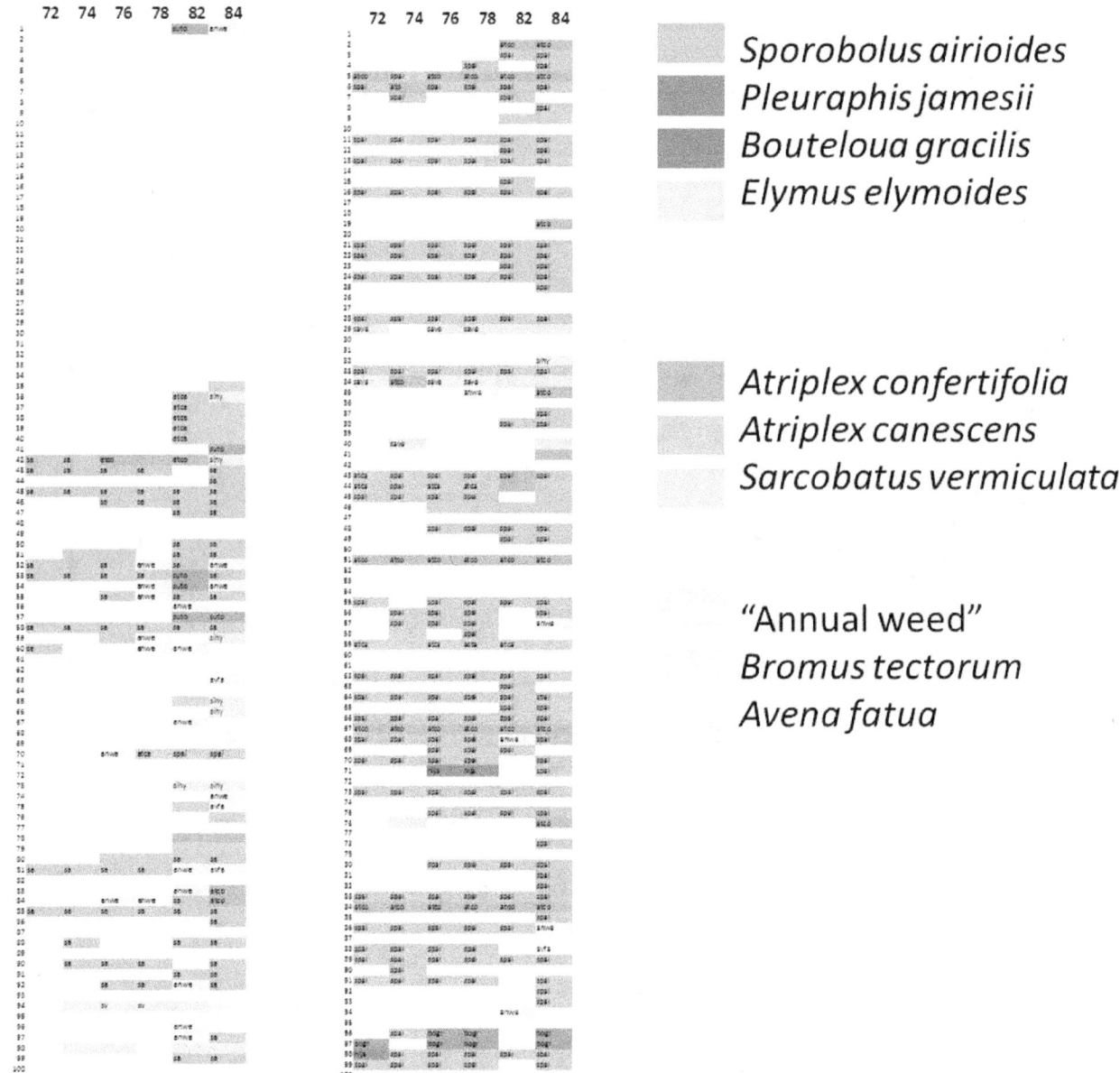

Figure 24. Diagram showing vegetation change along the Johnson transects (G Johnson, National Park Service, unpub. data, 1984). Rows are points on the transects, columns represent years. Basal cover is shown, except when there was no basal cover, canopy cover is shown. Rowlands did not document spatial information (P Rowlands, National Park Service, unpub. data, 1992), therefore, the 1992 data are omitted from this figure.

Vegetation Map Data

The total vegetative cover is clearly different between these two clusters (fig. 25*A*): the longer rested southern cluster has 50 percent greater vegetative cover than the northern cluster. Species richness is almost identical among the two clusters and the variance is large (fig. 25*B*). An NMDS ordination of species composition indicates a modest degree of separation among the clusters along the horizontal axis, the "northerliness" axis (fig. 25*C*). The most important species were identified as having an indicator value of greater than 25. The major correlates with the southern group— those fenced longer—were *B. gracilis* (*tau* = -0.38, P = 0.001), *P. jamesii* (*tau* = -0.32, P = 0.01), and *Salsola tragus* (*tau* = -0.49, P = 0.001). The major correlates with the northern group were *Isocoma drummondii* (*tau* = 0.40, P <0.0001) and *Parryella filifolia* (P = 0.03). *B. gracilis* and *P. jamesii*, although often thought of as grazing increasers, are two to three times more abundant in the longer rested southern cluster. Surprisingly, *Salsola* spp. also is more strongly associated with longer rest in this data, although it tends to be associated with less vegetated, erosion prone landscapes. It is difficult to to interpret the association of *I. drummondii* and *P. filifolia* with the more recently fenced northern cluster. Both are known from more sandy habitats, and the germination of *I. drummondii* is suppressed by salt (Baskin and Baskin, 1998) suggesting that this may have more to do with gradients of sand deposition than grazing, a hypothesis that we cannot rule out for any of these patterns.

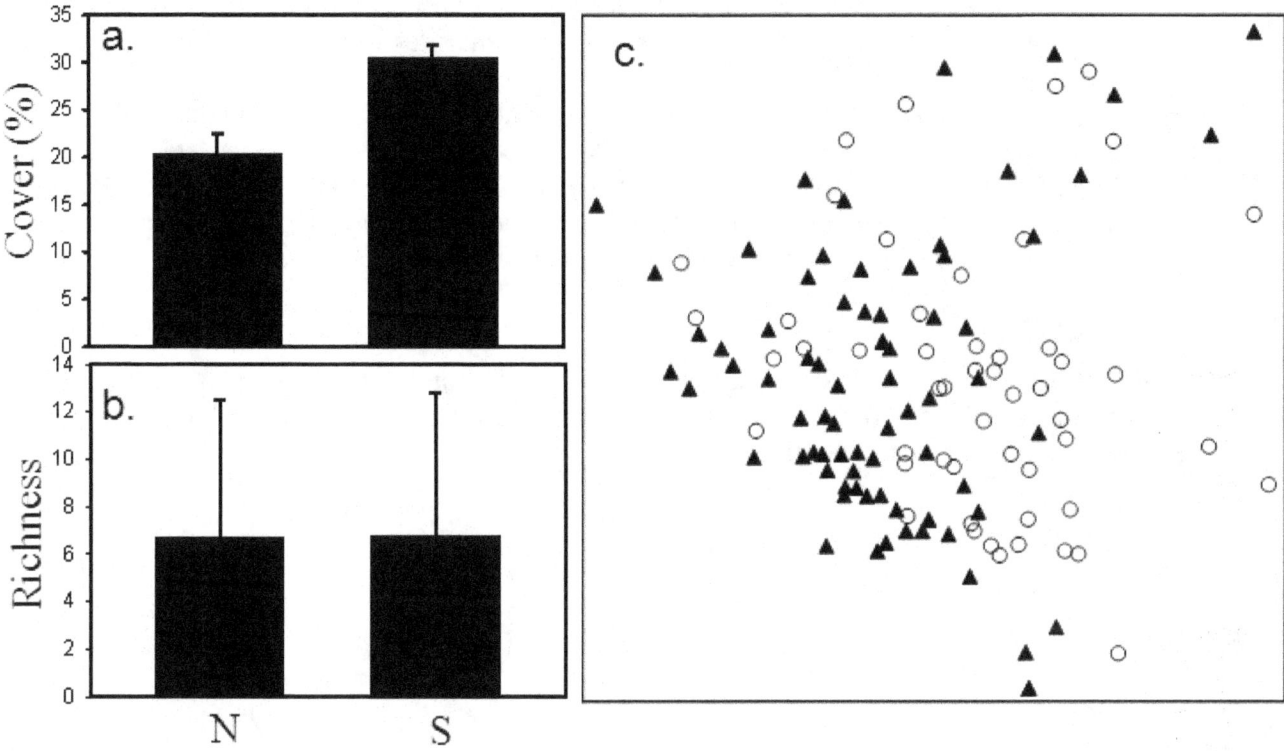

Figure 25. Graphs showing vegetational differences among northern (fenced later) and southern (fenced earlier) clusters of Clayey fans sampling sites (Thomas and others, 2009). (*A*) Cover is approximately 50 percent greater in the southern cluster. (*B*) Richness does not differ. (*C*) An NMDS ordination showing a moderate degree of separation between northern and southern clusters in unrelativized vegetation composition. The horizontal axis represents northerliness.

Grazing Dynamics

Despite that both analyses of grazing dynamics have flaws, we can draw some tentative inferences *based on the agreement between these two datasets*. There is much uncertainty in drawing these conclusions, but they are based on the best evidence available:

1. The data do not strongly support that *S. airioides* is a grazing decreaser any more than other community members. Like the majority of species, its abundance seems to be lower when time since grazing is shorter, however, it may act to facilitate the establishment of vegetated patches. There is no landscape-wide difference in abundance for this species among northern and southern clusters of sites.
2. Likewise, the data do not strongly support that *B. gracilis* or *P. jamesii* are grazing increasers in this ecological site. They were largely absent from Johnson's transects in 1972, and they are distinctly more abundant in the southern cluster of the sites from Thomas and others (2009), which have been fenced longer.
3. The most obvious putative effect of grazing is that cover can increase dramatically when grazing ceases. This demonstrates a large degree of resilience in this ecosystem to grazing.
4. There is no evidence that *E. nauseosa* or *G. sarothhrae* increase in the presence of grazing or decrease in its absence, in this ecological site. *E. nauseosa* may be common near streams, but otherwise both of these species are lesser influences.

Cluster Analysis

We selected a seven-cluster solution (fig. 26), which can be illustrated in an ordination. Our ordination was three-dimensional. Many clusters separated relatively cleanly, although viewing all three axes is necessary to see the separation.

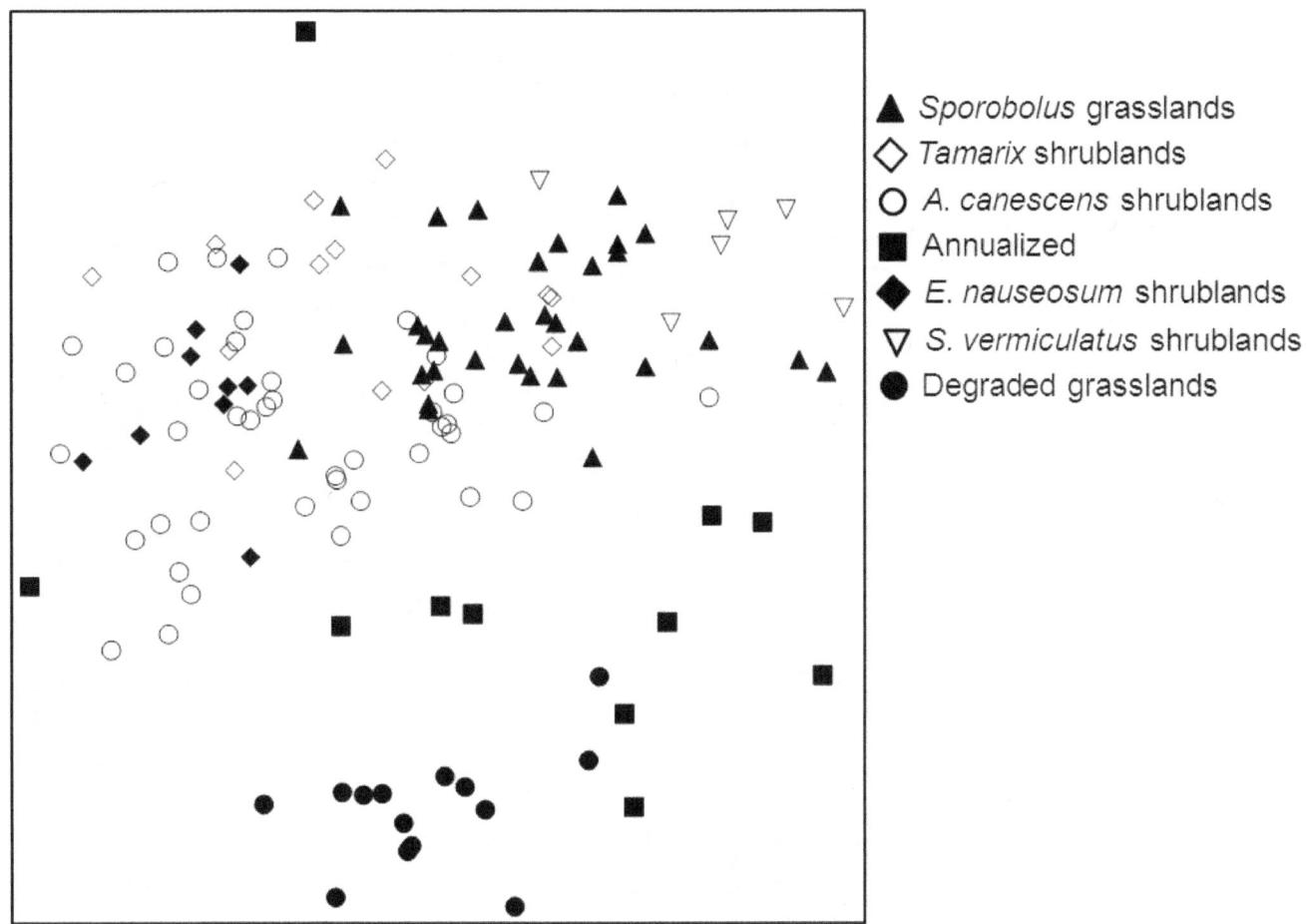

Figure 26. Diagram of non-metric multidimensional scaling ordination of a seven-cluster solution in the first two of three dimensions.

Based on the seven-cluster solution, we determined the degree of correlation of various species with the clusters (fig. 27). We determined there were clusters indicated well by: (1) *A. obovata* and *S. airoides*, (2) *Tamarix* spp., (3) *A. canescens*, (4) *E. nauseosa*, (5) *Opuntia polycarpa*, *B, tectorum*, and various forbs, and (6) *Sarcobatus vermiculatus*. One cluster has no good indicators, possibly suggesting high variability. However, all species that were best associated with this cluster were annuals including *Bromus madritensis* and *Salsola* spp.

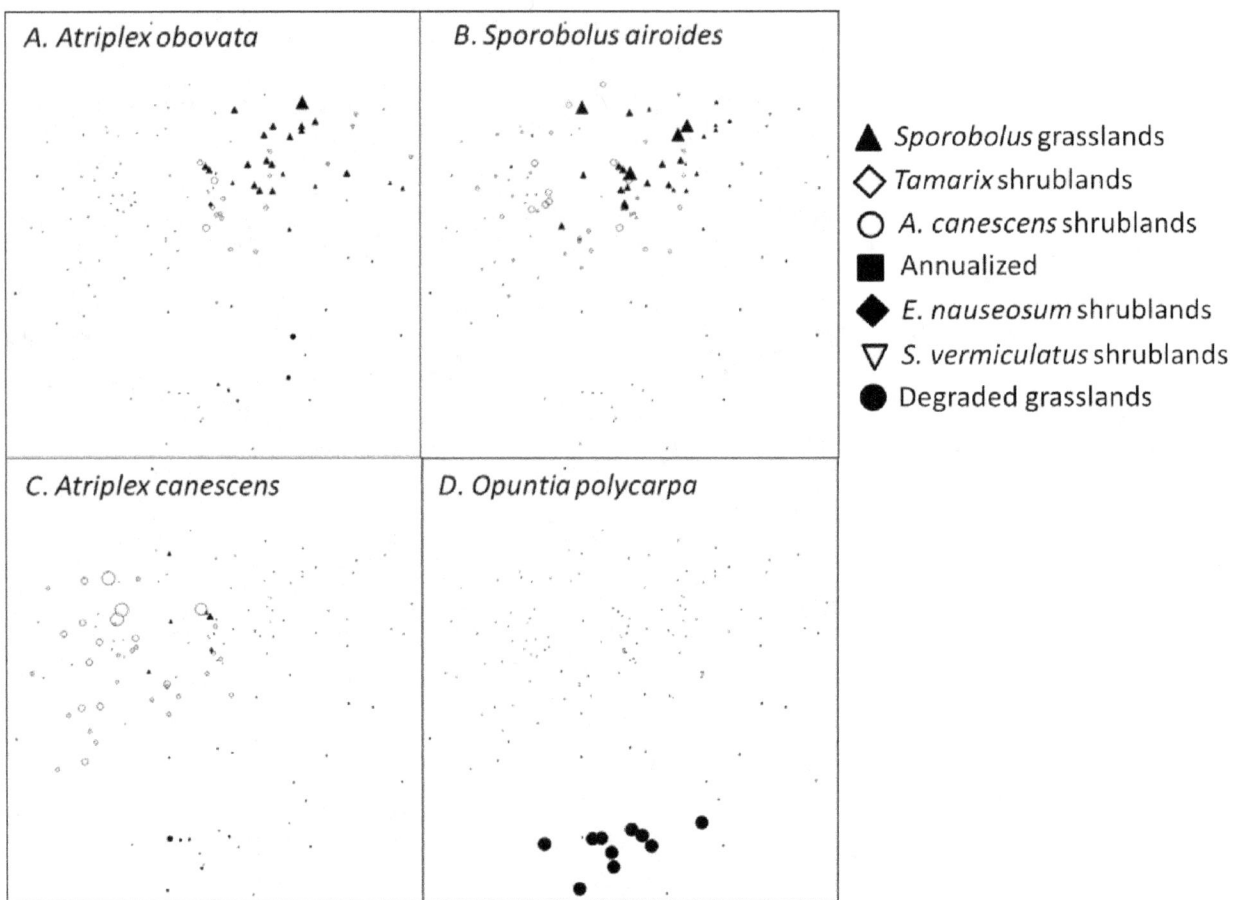

Figure 27. Diagram showing four versions of the above NMDS ordination, illustrating some of the indicator species of the various clusters. In each panel, the symbols are resized based on the abundance of a single species or biotic component. It is clear that particular species correlate well with particular clusters. (*A*) *A. obovata*, an indicator of grasslands. (*B*) *S. airoides* an indicator of grasslands. (*C*) *A. canescens* an indicator of *A. canescens* shrublands. (*D*) *Opuntia polycarpa* an indicator of degraded grasslands.

Final State-and-Transition Model

Based on our analysis of grazing dynamics and cluster analysis, we finalized our STM (fig. 28).

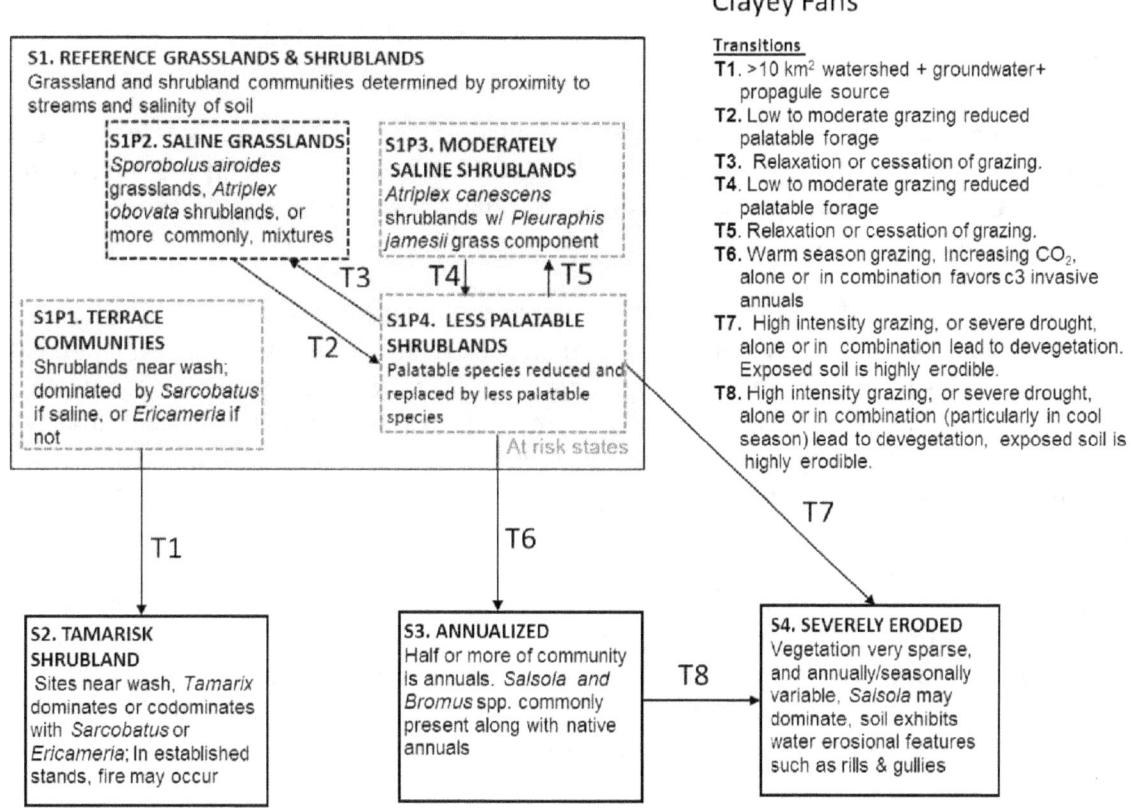

Clayey Fans

Transitions
T1. >10 km² watershed + groundwater+ propagule source
T2. Low to moderate grazing reduced palatable forage
T3. Relaxation or cessation of grazing.
T4. Low to moderate grazing reduced palatable forage
T5. Relaxation or cessation of grazing.
T6. Warm season grazing, Increasing CO₂, alone or in combination favors c3 invasive annuals
T7. High intensity grazing, or severe drought, alone or in combination lead to devegetation. Exposed soil is highly erodible.
T8. High intensity grazing, or severe drought, alone or in combination (particularly in cool season) lead to devegetation, exposed soil is highly erodible.

Figure 28. State-and-transition diagram for Clayey fans. Boxes represent states, arrows represent possible transitions and dashed boxes represent phases within states.

Catalog of States and Phases

S1. Reference grasslands and shrublands: Miller (1975) suggested that a "climax" community is most likely to consist of *S. airoides* (15–30 percent), *B. gracilis* (15–25 percent), *P. jamesii* (10–15 percent), and *E. nauseosa* (10–15 percent). Based on typical response of community members to grazing, it was proposed that *B. gracilis*, *P. jamesii*, and *Sprobolus heterolepsis* would be expected to increase proportionally. The current ecological site description acknowledges a shrub component in the potential vegetation state, primarily *A. canescens*, and does not consider *E. nauseosa* an important "climax" community member. It goes on to suggest that the most likely increasers are *G. sarothrae*, *E. nauseosa*, cacti (presumably *Opuntia*), and annuals. We conducted an analysis of two datasets that failed to document these increaser-decreaser behaviors. Rather, putative grazing impacts seem to reduce all species, and the dominance structure is fairly similar in more and less recently grazed sites.

We acknowledge an important spatial mosaic determined by two abiotic factors that are partially independent: salinity and distance from a wash. Clayey fans are alluvial features and thus contain washes. Near washes, local dominance of *S. vermiculatus* or *E. nauseosa*, with various codominants is possible but does not cover a large area (Thomas and others, 2009). More distant from the wash we find a spatial mosaic of *A. obovata*, *P. jamesii*, and *S. airoides* communities, and *A. canescens*, *Pleuraphis jamesii* communities. Only occasionally are true *S. airoides* grasslands observed in small patches despite greater than 40 years of rest from grazing (Thomas and others, 2009). Intermediates between these four scenarios are likely to occur as well. DeCoster and Swan (2009a) list *S. airoides*, *A. obovata*, and *P. jamesii* as the three most abundant species, but the high standard deviation in cover supports the assertion that there is a large degree of spatial heterogeneity.

S1 Phase1. Terrace communities: This spatial phase occurs on infrequently active, stable terraces near washes. They are shrublands, either dominated by *S. vermiculatus* when saline, or *E. nauseosa* when less saline. Based on their palatability, *Sarcobatus* communities are susceptible to degradation whereas *E. nauseosa* communities are likely to be resistant.

S1 Phase2. Saline grasslands: This spatial phase occurs close to or distant from washes, and its soils may be more strongly influenced by the parent materials for the Chinle Formation relative to other materials. This assertion is inferential and based on the fact that Chinle parent materials are saline, and there is a salinity tolerance gradient in potential plant communities. This phase would be dominated by *A. obovata* (a salinity tolerant shrub; Hodgekinson 1987) either exclusively or accompanied by *P. jamesii* and *S. airoides* (a salinity tolerant grass; Ungar, 1966). Pure stands of *S. airoides* are possible but much less common.

S1 Phase3. Moderately saline shrublands: This spatial phase occurs close to or distant from washes, and its soils may be less strongly influenced by the parent materials from the Chinle formation mixture with other materials. These tend to support shrublands of *A. canescens* with a herbaceous component dominated by *P. jamesii*. These species are salt tolerant but less so than *A. obovatum* and *S. airoides* (Hodgekinson, 1987; Natural Resources Conservation Service, 2010).

S1 Phase4. Less palatable shrublands: Cover is sharply reduced in the majority of species. Differences in relative species composition attributable to grazing are not obvious (see analysis). *B. tectorum* and various perennial forbs and subshrubs may be important community members. Due to reduced buffering of erosive forces by vegetation, this state is likely subject to water erosion. The state retains resilience as long as *S. airoides* is still present.

S2. Tamarisk shrubland: This state is documented by Thomas and others (2009) especially near the Puerco River (Thomas and others 2003), although it is not a major community type on the landscape. These invaded shrublands may emerge due to replacement of *E. nauseosa* (Ladenburger and others, 2006), and because of the phreatophytic characteristics of *Tamarix* spp., they are unlikely to occur distant from stream channels. This state will be possible if the watershed is at least 10 km^2 and has some degree of persistent alluvial groundwater (Shaw and Cooper, 2008). If high density is attained, these communities can burn, reinforcing dominance of the resprouting *Tamarix* spp. Additionally, *Tamarix* spp. localizes salts at the soil surface in its leaf litter, making colonization by less tolerant species more difficult. For these reasons, this state tends to reinforce itself. As ecological site descriptions and mapping abilities become more refined, we may find that these communities actually represent a different ecological site.

S3. Annualized: This state is highly dominated or codominated by the invasive exotic forb *Salsola* spp. Seasonally, these can be productive, and dead tumbleweeds can afford some degree of protection against erosive forces. Sites such as these may be seasonally susceptible to water erosion because *Salsola* spp. cover may be sparse.

S4. Severely eroded: This state is largely theoretical. These fluvial-alluvial soils contain a substantial proportion of clays from the Chinle Formation as source material. These bentonitic, shrink-swell clays have a very poor degree of stability when wet because aggregates expand, destroying the structure (Bowker and others, 2008). When such soils are lacking in biological soil crust development, as indicated by DeCoster and Swan (2009a) in the case in Petrified Forest National Park, their aggregate stability tends to only be around 1.7 (Bowker and others, 2008) using the Herrick soil aggregate stability test (Herrick and others, 2001). DeCoster and Swan (2009a) report a higher value for interspaces, about 3.7, suggesting that some sites with less proportional abundance of bentonitic clay, and therefore more stability, exist, or that there is undetected and highly cryptic colonization by cyanobacteria conferring some stability. These soils are prone to forming physical crusts when dry (DeCoster and Swan, 2009a), which resist wind erosion. A severely eroded state would be expected to have very poor plant cover, possible dominance by vegetation that is only seasonal such as *Salsola* spp., and clear evidence of active water erosion such as rills and gullies. This would be especially likely on sloping sites.

Transitions and Threshold Estimation

Transition 6: S1P4 Less palatable shrublands to S3 Annualized

Transition 6 can be modeled by the logistic function, with a pseudo R^2 of 0.53:

$$\text{probability of transition} = \tag{15}$$

$$1/1 +e -(2.9988 – 0.2019(\text{percent total plant cover}))$$

According to this equation, as total vegetation cover falls to about 29 percent this transition becomes possible (5 percent probability). At 20 percent and 14.5 percent cover, the transition becomes 25 and 50 percent probable. Near certainty (95 percent probability) of transition is not observed until plant cover is 0 (fig. 29).

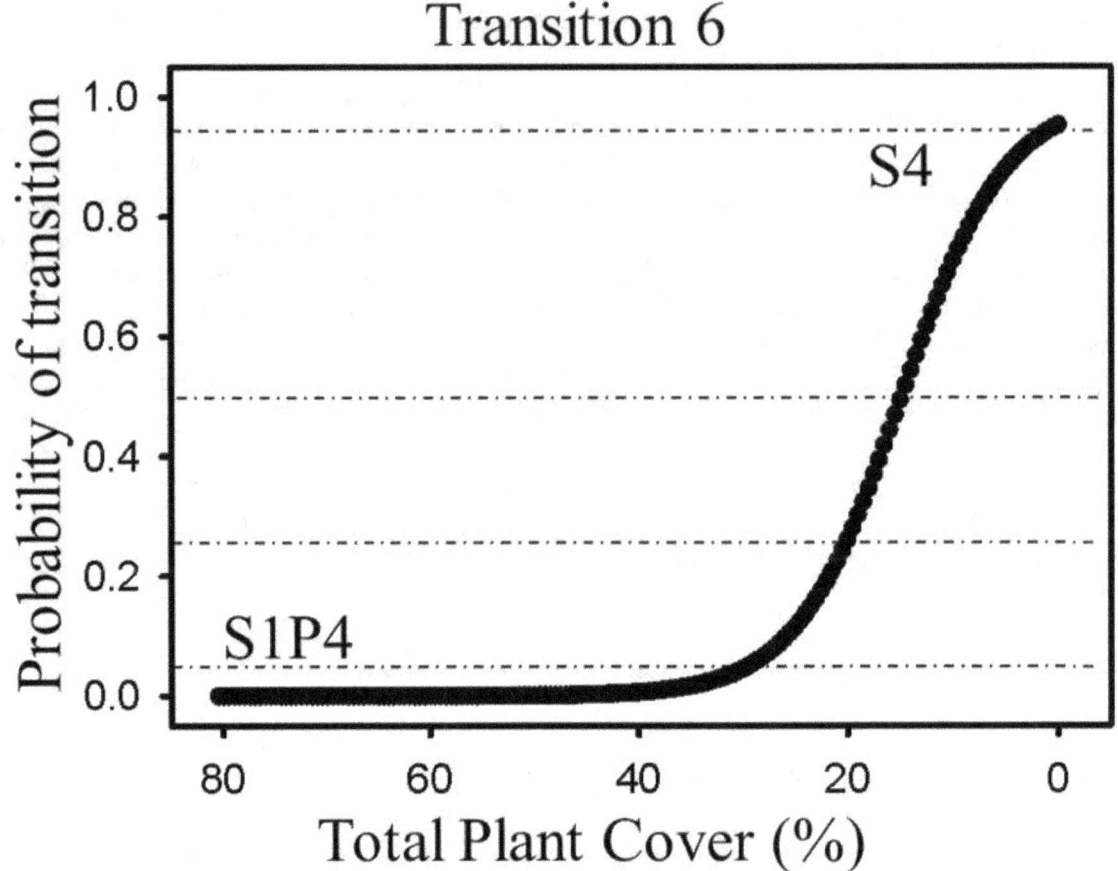

Figure 29. Modeled probabilities of transition from S1P4 Less palatable shrublands to S4 Severely eroded, given a range of total plant cover. Dashed lines represent critical probabilities (5 percent, 25 percent, 50 percent, 95 percent).

Interpretation

Our analyses suggest Clayey fans to be a naturally spatially heterogeneous mix of different plant communities. Datasets examined captured various phases or spatial variants, but clear alternative states are only weakly documented. This is likely because all data are from within Petrified Forest National Park, which has been a low disturbance environment over the last several decades. A better understanding of alternative states and corresponding transitions and thresholds may be possible if data were collected outside of the park in degraded areas, where Clayey fans may have transitioned to *Tamarix* shrublands, become annualized, or are experiencing unchecked erosion.

The one exception was transition 6 from S1 Phase 2 to S3. The putative annualized state, S3, is actually difficult to define. The state has no characteristic species but is characterized by overall low cover, and multiple exotic annuals may be major parts of the community—though the dominant exotics may differ from site to site. We provide a tentative analysis based on total plant cover, but acknowledge that a better understanding of S3 would benefit the estimation of thresholds in this ecological site.

Case Study 7: Limy Uplands

Background

Limy uplands are an ecological site represented in Wupatki National Monument and surrounding areas, situated atop fairly level basalt flows, receiving 15.2–25.4 cm of rainfall per year (Soil Conservation Service, 1983). The soil is weathered in place from the underlying basalt and from later cinder deposits due to regional volcanism. The surface is gravelly because of a large amount of surface cinder coverage. Grassland vegetation is most common and is dominated by C4 rhizomatous or stoloniferous grasses including *Pleuraphis jamesii* and *Bouteloua eriopoda*; C3 grasses may have been somewhat diminished because of past grazing. Savanna vegetation is less common and is characterized by an overstory of *Juniperus monosperma* of varying density and an understory of perennial grasses (Jameson, 1962; Ironside, 2006; DeCoster and Swan, 2009b).

The primary management goals of Wupatki National Monument are to protect and preserve more than 2,000 catalogued archeological sites, including structures, and agricultural fields of the ancient ancestral Hopi cultures, and to provide interpretive and educational experiences for park visitors (National Park Service, 2002). Grazing was permitted in portions of the monument until 1989 when livestock were removed and a boundary fence was constructed (National Park Service, 2002). Wupatki National Monument highlights the presence of a rare, large, currently ungrazed grassland as one of its significant resources, and NPS staff are concerned that increasing tree densities in the monument grasslands are attributable to a decrease in fire frequency since the late 19th century caused by diminished fine fuels from grazing (Cinnamon, 1988; National Park Service, 2002; Ironside, 2006). Currently, the wildfire management plan calls for suppression of fires, but retains the option of prescribed fire (National Park Service, 2005).

Methods

A Priori State-and-Transition Model

Based on a thorough literature review, we developed an *a priori* state and transition model. We prepared a figure, and a detailed catalog of states and phases of the *a priori* model for reference in expert opinion surveys. Due to a history of volcanism and long-term human occupation, appropriate reference vegetative communities in Wupatki should be defined with care. Here we emphasize what is likely possible under management scenarios today (2013). Paleoecological studies could potentially suggest reference communities from a variety of time periods, some of which are not possible under current climate regimes. Some are not possible under current conditions. States are divided into pre-historic and historic-modern (manageable) to make this distinction. We focus on historical modern states.

Data

Relevant vegetation data for this ecological site either are well-replicated and incomplete, or modestly replicated and reasonably complete. In aggregate, these data may not represent a sufficient range of the possible states, nor the ideal time series data capturing a transition in action to validate a STM, and may lack measurements of some potentially useful indicators. There is no single complete dataset, for validation of a STM or estimation of tipping and assessment points. Hassler (2006) likely conducted some sampling of *J. monosperma* density, growth rate, and fire mortality on Limy uplands, but individual sample locations are not documented. In a remote sensing-based vegetation mapping project, Hansen and others (2004) sampled numerous accuracy assessment releves in limy uplands that qualitatively identify community type. Miller and others (2007) developed and tested monitoring techniques at seven plots. DeCoster and Swan (2009b) summarize the first years of the I&M program and contains the most purposefully collected monitoring dataset for Limy uplands, but is limited to 10 sites. The randomly selected study design may fortuitously capture recovery from fire gradients (one plot in 1995, "North fire"; three to four plots in the 2002, "Antelope fire"; USDI-NPS, 2005). The data include detailed information on vegetation structure and ground cover, including some metrics of juniper density, but lacks direct indices of connectivity of fine fuels.

Expert Opinion Surveys

Because of the incomplete nature of the available data, we pursued an alternative strategy for the validation of the states and dynamics delineated in the STM. We constructed email-based questionnaires in two phases: (1) model calibration, and (2) estimation of tipping and assessment points in indicators that enable detection of proximity to threshold crossings. We identified a list of potential expert consultants from the authors of relevant literature, and from professional interactions. We initially contacted selected experts by email to gauge interest, sent them surveys and recived them back. We revised the model, according to respondent comments and calculated an aggregate confidence value. The second phase of the survey was more focused on thresholds associated with a key transition (from reference grasslands to savannized ecosystems). We emailed the phase 2 surveys to respondents who had previously returned phase 1 surveys, in addition to several previous candidates who had not been able to respond. Survey format is documented in appendix A.

Results

Final State and Transition Model

We collected responses from four reviewers of the phase 1 survey, and applied their suggestions in the following ways to finalize our STM (fig. 29). We added the possibility of a woodland state, a transition based on persistent wet conditions, which is a plausible although not probable global change scenario. Only one respondent, with modest confidence, suggested this change. In the Rhizomatous grasslands (S1) and Savannized (S2) states, we delineated a separate shrub-dominated phase. Previously, the "denuded" state was a catch-all that could mean shrub-dominated or devegetated. Two respondents, with moderate confidence, suggested that these states should be defined separately. In the lengthier, verbal description of the model, we made several minor changes. We provide some qualifications about interpreting palynological and midden data. We broadened description of human occupation impacts; previously just dry farming activities were mentioned. We speculated on the potential grass cover in S1, and whether current conditions (about 20 years without grazing) have attained it. We acknowledged that *Salsola* spp. could play a role in *J. monosperma* fire susceptibility, observed by Jameson (1962) but we are not aware of *Salsola* spp. dominated states in this ecological site, so no states or phases were added. However, increasing *Salsola* spp. prevalence has been observed over time, so such a state may become possible (DeCoster, National Park Service, oral commun., 2011.). We clearly distinguish livestock grazing from native browsing. We acknowledge that pronghorn (*A. americana*) browsing can trigger transitions from shrub-dominance to grass-dominance, and that past low points in pronghorn populations could have contributed to savannization or other woody plant dominance. We added a few details to clarify the S3 state. We acknowledge that different grass communities might be possible in S1, for example *Pleuraphis*-only, *Bouteloua*-only, or bunchgrass-dominated; however, to keep the model simple, we do not add additional phases. We removed language describing savannization as "*Juniperus* invasion," because it implies that *Juniper* does not belong in this ecosystem when this is not known with certainty.

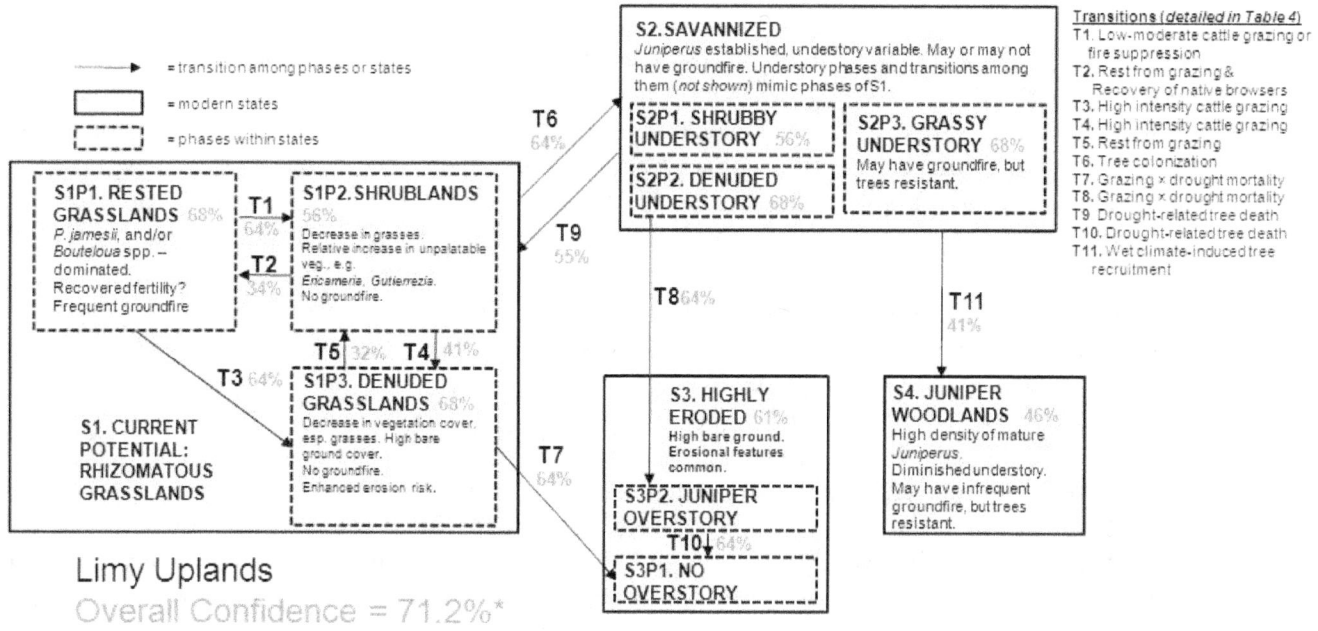

Figure 30. A state-and-transition model for Limy uplands of Wupatki and surrounding areas. Aggregate confidence values are in gray. * = The overall confidence estimate applies to all states and phases, except those for which an additional estimate is shown.

Catalog of States and Phases—Final STM

S1. Current potential: rhizomatous grasslands: This state consists of potentially grass-dominated ecosystems. Preferential grazing of grasses may lead to a higher prevalence of shrubs; and excessive grazing may lead to dramatic decreases in plant biomass. This state retains the resilience to recover from such perturbances.

S1 Phase1. Rested grasslands: Prior to the initiation of grazing the area had more than 500 years to recover from agricultural disturbance. We know little about this period, except that midden analysis suggests that relative abundance of plant macrofossils does not appear to have changed much over this time. Presumably cover increased. Potential cover is about equal to or greater than the current average of 15 percent, after 20 years of rest from grazing (Miller and others, 2007; DeCoster and Swan, 2009b). The range assessment also suggests a greater prevalence of bunchgrass species in this phase and a lesser prevalence of the rhizomatous *P. jamesii* and *Bouteloua* spp. based on prevailing ideas regarding increaser-decreaser plants at that time (Doughty, 1971). Midden evidence suggests that *H. comata* (a tussock grass) may well have been more important in the past, but the present rhizomatous dominants, *Bouteloua* spp. and *P. jamesii,* also were well-represented macrofossils from that time. These major species may occur alone or in various combinations; in a more detailed model, these might be considered separate phases. The supposedly frequent ground fire interval (Cinnamon, 1988; Hassler, 2006) would tend to favor the rhizomatous species, such as *P. jamesii* and *Bouteloua* spp. (Jameson,

1962; Ford, 1999). This fire return cycle also likely discouraged shrub and tree colonization, conferring resistance to state change in this phase.

S1 Phase2. Shrublands: In the late 1800s, livestock grazing was introduced (Jameson, 1962), and its intensity peaked early in the 20th century. Based on general knowledge of behavior of common plant species under livestock grazing, the *relative* abundance of palatable grasses, such as *H. comata* or *A. hymenoides,* would be expected to decrease, and unpalatable shrub species such as *G. sarothrae* and *E. nauseosa* or grazing tolerant grass species, such as *Bouteloua gracilis,* might increase. Livestock grazing decreases the standing biomass of fine fuels and their connectivity, decreasing the susceptibility of this system to fire. This in turn allows more *J. monosperma* recruits to invade. Invasion by *Salsola* spp. also may be possible at this stage. The fire cycle that maintains S1P1 (rested grasslands) can be strongly compromised, making this phase at-risk of further change. However, due to resprout of rhizomatous grasses, and dietary preference of shrubs over grasses of native browsers (Jacques and others, 2006), it displays considerable resilience.

S1 Phase3. Denuded grasslands: This removal of biomass described in S1P2 (shrublands) can proceed to extreme levels (fig. 30, left panel). This state is dominated by unvegetated bare ground. The vegetation that remains resembles S1P2. Because of resprout ability of rhizomatous grasses, and a feeding preference of shrubs over grasses in native grazers (pronghorn), this phase displays resilience despite its appearance. Sites in similar condition were known to have recovered much productivity.

Figure 31. Photographs showing (left panel) an extreme version of S1P3 (denuded grasslands) in 1907 and (right panel) S2 (savannized) in 1961. Photographs do not appear to be specifically on Limy Uplands but provide some insight regarding the general dynamics of these grasslands. (Photographs from Jameson, 1962; 1907 photographer is unidentified and 1961 photographer is presumed to be D. Jameson, U.S. Forest Service.)

S2. Savannized: To date, Limy uplands have been less susceptible to juniper encroachment than surrounding areas but it is clear that the prevalence of juniper in increasing in the grasslands and former grasslands of Wupatki (Cinnamon, 1988; Hassler, 2006; Ironside, 2006; Parker, 2009). A comparison of basalt soils to limestone soils indicated that tree growth rate or density did not differ, but average age of establishment occurred later on basaltic soils (Hassler, 2006). There is sufficient rooting depth, but perhaps the soil texture challenges the junipers ability to colonize delaying the process (Bowker and others, 2012b). Simulation modeling based on 20th century climate regimes indicate that Limy uplands have a high probability of *J. monosperma* colonization (Ironside, 2006), if that climate regime were to continue. If grazing keeps fines fuels low, fire cannot cull colonizing junipers making savannization likely. Periods of wet weather conditions also can conceivably favor *J. monosperma* recruitment. Savannized states consist of at least three phases based on the condition of the understory and fire behavior. These phases and the transitions among them mimic the phases of State 1.

S2 Phase1. Denuded understory: Understory and fire susceptibility (low) is similar to S1P3 (denuded grasslands).

S2 Phase 2. Shrubby understory: Understory and fire susceptibility (low) is similar to S1P2 (unpalatable shrublands).

S2 Phase3. Grassy understory: Understory and fire susceptibility (high) is similar to S1P1 (rested grasslands). Tree death is unlikely during fires (Hassler, 2006), except in the rare case of accumulation of *Salsola* spp. at tree base (Jameson, 1962).

S3. Highly eroded: If heavy grazing continues unabated, or if a severe drought occurred during a denuded phase of S1 or S2, a transition to a severely eroded state is possible. This state is theoretical in that sites in Wupatki were known to have been strongly denuded, yet subsequently recovered (fig. 5). A state such as this would require persistent loss of much vegetation (that is, mortality) due to trampling and heavy grazing, drought, or both. This state is dominated by bare ground and would be characterized by erosional features such as rills, gullies, terracettes, and sheeting. Although the cinder-covered surface and generally flat slopes are inherent properties of this ecological site that lend it low-erosion potential, such a reduction in vegetation cover could conceivably initiate erosion, because water-stable aggregate structure of exposed soil surface is very poor (generally less than 2 using Herrick soil stability test; Bowker and Belnap, 2007). This state would be maintained because high erosion rates prevent revegetation, and the lack of vegetation prevents stabilization of soil.

S3 Phase1. No overstory: This phase occurs when the transition precedes savannization, or when S3P2 (highly eroded-Juniper overstory) loses its trees from drought.

S3 Phase 2. Juniper overstory: This phase occurs when the erosion is initiated, post-savannization.

S4. Juniper woodlands: This state is largely theoretical as mapped Limy uplands currently do not support woodlands. There is perhaps an analog on Powerline Mesa (Hassler, 2006), south of Wupatki National Monument, a woodland on a basalt shelf less than 100 m higher than the Limey uplands. Tree age is much older compared to savannas, suggesting that such woodlands require centuries to develop, and that they developed before grazing. This site is not covered in any published soil surveys, thus its ecological site designation is not known. Although many future climate projections suggest unfavorable conditions for *J. monosperma* in the current century (Ironside, 2006), there is much uncertainty in these projections, and climate change scenarios that enhance moisture availability could lead to the development of a *J. monosperma* woodland (Phase 1 respondent, written commun.). Woodlands are distinguished from savannas by increased tree density, and a diminished grass understory due to shading and tree litter deposition.

Confidence—Final STM

Overall confidence in this STM was estimated at about 71 percent, meaning that although empirical evidence is somewhat sparse, respondents tended to believe that the model captures the ecosystem dynamics. The lowest confidences were associated with the existence of and transition to a woodland state. This is because only one respondent suggested the inclusion of this state, with modest confidence. We suggest this is an area deserving of further study.

Transitions and Threshold Estimation

We were able to obtain threshold estimates for five indicators from a minimum of three respondents (table 5). To avoid making the survey so difficult that respondents would not complete it, we built some flexibility in that they could choose which indicators to provide thresholds. Confidence is estimates averaged between about 25 and 40, and maximal confidence estimates were usually about 50 percent.

Table 5. Threshold estimates for five indicators of the transition from reference states to savannized states.
[Average and maximal confidence and number of respondents can all be considered measures of estimate quality]

Indicators	Assessment point	Mean adj. confidence	Maximal adj. confidence	Number of respondents	Tipping point	Mean adj. confidence	Maximal adj. confidence	Number of respondents
time since fire (y)	22.4	37 percent	48 percent	4	28.0	40 percent	48 percent	3
total plant cover (percent)	18.8	40 percent	51 percent	6	7.7	39 percent	51 percent	5
basal cover incl. litter (percent)	17	38 percent	51 percent	5	9.7	37 percent	51 percent	4
interspace length (cm)	66.7	42 percent	42 percent	4	-	-	-	-
average tree height (m)	0.86	42 percent	42 percent	3	1.62	27 percent	42 percent	3

Our survey used the terms "assessment point" and "tipping point"; the former is the point at which a management action should be considered to avert an undesired state transition, and the latter is the point at which a transition has occurred or is imminent.

Interpretation

These surveys provide a first approximation of events that might trigger management actions. They suggest that a management action (for example, prescribed fire, tree removal, reduction of grazing) ought to occur if about 22 years have passed without a wildland fire (for example, prescribed fire), if total plant cover decreases to less than about 18 percent or basal cover and litter cover decreases to less than 17 percent or interspace length exceeds about 67 cm (reduction of native or livestock grazing, manipulation of water sources, restoration seeding), or average tree height exceeds about 0.9 m (prescribed fire, tree removal). The surveys also provide some definition of the actual boundary between the grassland and savannized states. Savannized states will have gone about 28 years or more without fire, plant canopy cover is lower than about 8 percent and summed basal and litter cover decreases to less than about 10 percent, and trees average at least 1.62 m.

Clearly these estimates should be verified with empirical data if possible, preferably experimental. However, lacking such resources we are still able to generate some rough guidelines for anticipating possible threshold crossings. Because most ecological sites are likely to fall in this data-sparse category, we should not overlook expert opinion as a means of acquiring information about probable ecosystem dynamics.

Discussion

Our operational approach to evaluating threshold dynamics for upland ecological sites in dryland systems offers a variety of advantages:

1. State-and-transition models for individual ecological sites specifically articulate hypotheses regarding reference conditions and ecosystem dynamics in the context of goals for management and monitoring.

Attributes of alternative states help to identify biophysical features that may be indicators of an impending transition (threshold crossing). Listing known or hypothesized mechanisms and processes underlying transitions among alternative states and phases also aids in identifying indicators to be monitored. This helps guide quantitative and qualitative estimation of tipping points and establishment of assessment points for monitoring purposes. In dryland systems, resource managers use ecological sites to stratify sampling in monitoring programs because of the likelihood that dynamics will vary among ecological site types (for example, Herrick and others, 2005; O'Dell and others, 2005; Thomas and others, 2006). Applying STMs and associated threshold-related assessments to individual ecological sites provides results specific to individual ecosystems and their unique management challenges.

2. This approach enables monitoring for focused management decision making, by narrowing the breadth of information to monitor.

Theoretically, the number of possible threshold triggers affecting an ecological site and resulting pathways can be unlimited. In developing a STM, there is a natural rendering of this unlimited number to those known to occur from past observation or perceived to be highly plausible based on logic and deductive reasoning (that is, experience with other dryland systems or ecological site types). This more limited and practical domain is more understandable by managers, and preventative and remediation actions can be prescribed for specific conditions and alternative states. Furthermore, explicit consideration of key change agents and associated management actions in STMs promotes monitoring for management decision making (Nichols and Williams, 2006). A major barrier to monitoring for active conservation is a lack of explicit representations of hypotheses about ecosystem responses to management actions, climate, and other drivers of ecosystem dynamics. Formalizing current system knowledge in STMs is an initial and critical step for focused discussion and understanding of useful indicators for monitoring and for designing responsible and efficient monitoring efforts to inform management actions.

3. We provide a quantitative approach to estimate tipping and assessment points using data.

An ideal dataset for the estimation of assessment and tipping points would consist of a well-replicated experimental manipulation of stressors where quantitative sampling of multiple key indicators in a time series would capture the progression of a transition. Such data resources are the minority, whereas data using space-for-time replacement tend to be much more available. Within one or a few points in time, samples are obtained that represent spatially discrete examples of different states and phases. Because the transitions are not actually documented in the data, it is assumed that the hypothesized states and transitions articulated in the STM are the correct model of ecosystem dynamics; observed degraded states are assumed to have transitioned in the past from other states because of the model-specified mechanisms. Statistical assessments relying on cluster analysis and the quantification of differences among clusters defines state membership, and indicator values most useful for distinguishing among states represent operational tipping points. Assessment points for the identified indicators can be specified on the basis of the natural variation in the less degraded state. Identifying key indicators and status associated with vulnerable phases or threshold crossings enables managers and scientists to ascribe meaningful and useful assessment points to ensure detection of a changing resource and to provide sufficient response time to prevent resource degradation or loss. This approach can be applied to the majority of cases for which there are available data; the basic requirements are hypothesized ecosystem dynamics and datasets that are able to capture multiple ecosystem states.

A large proportion of the literature on estimation of ecological thresholds considers cases where thresholds are determined based on a single indicator. When a process truly has a single best indicator, this can be a completely satisfactory method. However, in studies which consider only one of multiple possible predictors, there could be a high degree of uncertainty in this estimate. In studies which do consider multiple indicators, our results indicate that multivariate modeling rather than building multiple univariate models is the superior approach to avoid obtaining a conflicting set of answers. One conceptual problem with interpreting such models is that the values of the predictors are often viewed as varying independently, that is, assumed to be independent. Thus a typical way of presenting results is to hold one variable constant at various levels while varying the other variable to determine thresholds. If indeed the multiple indicators are indicative of the same process, they are not independent. A predictive system of regressions (for example, a path model) can be highly useful in simulating sufficient data while constraining the range in possible values of predictors and ensures that these entities which are correlated in nature covary realistically in thresholds estimation.

Classification and clustering are techniques which seek, by various methods, to group datapoints into increasing homogenous assemblages. Clustering uses multiple types of data simultaneously to create groups. Thus it is a reasonably good match for validating state concepts in empirical datasets. However, it provides little direct quantitative information about how exactly the groupings differ. Classification is a process by which a larger grouping of data is split into two smaller sets of data, generally based on the values of one type of data at a time (De'ath and Fabricius, 2000). This approach may provide a set of quantitative classification rules (for example, if bare ground cover is less than 20 percent, and annual cover is less than 10 percent = S2). Classifications rules may provide rough estimates of key thresholds in indicators but are not entirely satisfactory for this purpose because the classification is based on a pattern rather than the underlying process which led to the pattern. We suggest that path analysis is a tool which can help us construct deterministic process-based models based on known ecosystem dynamics.

To a large degree, the operational definition of a threshold will determine the method used to detect it. Much emphasis has been placed recently on the definition, "points or zones of abrupt change in ecological relationships" (Ficetola and others, 2009, page 1075). This definition is derived largely from May's (1973) definition which refers to points or zones where there changes in the state of matter occur. Groffman and others, (2006, Page 1) provides a dual definition as the "point at which there is an abrupt change in an ecosystem quality, or where small changes in an environmental driver produce large responses in the ecosystem." Friedel (1991) considered thresholds to be spatio-temporal boundaries between alternative states. Similarly, Muradian (2001) considered them to be critical values of a driver variable at which state changes occur.

A handful of methods have emerged to identify thresholds under this array of definitions, and much depends on the abruptness of the threshold behavior. A common application has been the probability of occurrence of a species or extinction of a population as a function of various descriptors of habitat loss and fragmentation (for example, distance to edge, habitat cover; Ficetola and Denoel, 2009; Toms and Lesperance, 2003). Piecewise regression has emerged as a useful tool for this application because it determines at what point in a given predictor an abrupt change occurs in the behavior of the response variable as a function of the predictor. For example, the structure of a community may change precipitously as a function of distance from an edge to a point where it is no longer responsive to additional change in this habitat parameter (Toms and Lesperance, 2003). In a recent test using simulated datasets, Ficetola and Denoel (2009) assert that logistic regression is a poor tool for estimating ecological thresholds because they may not detect the correct "point or zone of abrupt change" and that both piecewise regression and general additive models may function better. We do not fully agree with this assertion because the choice of a proper statistical approach will depend on the operational definition of "ecological threshold" being used. Further, the logistic function *can* detect the boundaries of the zones of abrupt change but not using a 50 percent probability value, which instead is a reasonable estimate of the center point of this zone. The intuitiveness of applying logistic regression, which estimates a probability of an event occurring, may fit better into the state-and-transition framework wherein the investigator wishes to know the probability of a state transition. Thus, logistic regression should not be dismissed so easily in this context.

4. We provide a non-empirical, partially quantitative approach to modeling ecosystem dynamics and estimating tipping and assessment points in the absence of data.

We developed a practical, qualitative approach to developing STMs and describing system dynamics where empirical data are sparse or lacking. This may be the dominant, data-availability scenario in dryland ecological sites of the Colorado Plateau. To accommodate these situations, we developed a Delphi-like protocol to use expert opinion and experience of resource managers and scientists to develop a STM and to begin to identify system attributes of impending thresholds and of alternative states after a threshold crossing. The Delphi method is based on the principle that group judgment is more accurate than individual judgment. Delphi methods attempt to estimate an unknown quantity (for example probability of an event occurring) by asking an anonymous expert panel their opinions in isolation (Linstone and Turoff, 1975; Oliver, 2002). Multiple iterations allow respondents to change their answer, based on the anonymous responses of other members, until convergence is achieved on a single value or a narrower range of values. We used some of the principles of this approach but did not seek convergence. We used the respondents' confidence in their own responses as weights in a procedure analogous to model averaging. In this way, we arrived at quantitative estimates of assessment points and tipping points in a few indicators along a transition sequence in only one iteration. We found this method to be reasonably efficient, requiring only two months and two surveys; however, it was difficult to obtain sufficient information on most indicators. Further, rather than seeking consensus, confidence estimation provides an additional product measuring respondents' self-assessed level of uncertainty about an issue and identifies the most pressing needs for additional evidence.

We were reasonably successful in the case of Limy uplands at attracting interested respondents. However, there were fewer respondents willing to conduct surveys for other case studies such as Clayey fans and Sandstone uplands. Rather than directly emailing potential respondents, we directed them to a web-based survey. Potentially, the web-based survey is an improvement in the process; however, it cannot overcome a lack of interested respondents. Another difficulty is an overlap among experts and informed persons for the various ecological sites. Once a respondent had completed a survey, it was difficult to engage them again to complete a survey for a different ecological site. Despite these difficulties, this approach remains an option when data are lacking.

Critics of similar expert-opinion methods suggest that such approaches only serve to boost confidence in respondents' ignorance. However, the dominant practice in resource conservation tends to be based on the experiential knowledge of individuals, rather than high-quality data or organized group judgment (Cook and others, 2010). We present our expert-opinion protocol as an improvement over the experiential knowledge of individuals that can be applied to identify critical indicator levels in monitoring any ecosystem. This approach can be applied more quickly and cheaply than a scientific study, giving it much utility when time or funds are limiting. Weighted averages of group assessment and tipping point estimates provide an intermediate level of quantitative data quality, higher than individual judgment and lower than quantitative field and experimental data. We do not consider a model produced using this procedure to be final, rather it is a first iteration of a useful model which should be refined as more information becomes available. For example, estimates of model parameters can serve to inform prior information in later Bayesian estimation using data.

Applying Threshold Concepts to Monitoring

Current monitoring efforts by the National Park Service Inventory and Monitoring program networks were developed without the benefit of a clear way to detect vulnerable conditions and tipping points associated with ecological thresholds. This is simply because knowledge of these conditions and tipping points is lacking or fragmentary. Nevertheless these monitoring protocols are well-designed to be able to use new knowledge pertaining to threshold dynamics. Results of analyses using our approaches have the potential to provide a more credible basis for establishing assessment points for these monitoring efforts. Estimates of assessment point values are surprisingly rare in the literature (see Digiovinazzo and others, 2010), yet they seem crucial to the goal of applying threshold concepts to management problems. This goal is consistent with application of a preventive threshold: attaining an assessment point of one or more indicators could trigger regulation of "changes to patterns that make systems vulnerable to deterministic or event-driven change" so that the undesired transition never occurs (Bestelmeyer, 2006).

To the greatest degree practicable, our methods should capture the essential dynamics underlying the process which leads to a transition, rather than the pattern which emerges as a result. Because of the large variability among ecosystems and localities, and the varying efficacy and availability of various sets of indicators, it is valuable to model threshold behaviors based on multiple indicators. Reliance on multiple pieces of information allow flexibility and buffer against uncertainty in the quality or utility in any one indicator (Pyke and others, 2002). To the greatest degree possible, we should retain the predictive power of proximate causal agents of a transition. These will be most tightly related to the phenomenon we wish to forecast or avoid. To anticipate transitions while they are still avoidable, we should retain information regarding upstream, less proximate causes. Path analysis for prediction provides one method for integrating the preceding principles.

In conservation and resource management, decisions must often be made regardless of the level of confidence in our knowledge of ecosystems (Soulé, 1985; Cook and others, 2010). Our goal should be to develop the best set of models possible given the level of information available to support decisions. The approaches presented here offer a flexible means of achieving this goal and determining specific research areas in need of study.

Acknowledgments

This work was supported by funding from the U.S. Geological Survey (Status and Trends of Biological Resources Program and Southwest Biological Science Center), the National Park Service (NPS) Northern and Southern Colorado Plateau Iventory Monitoring programs, and The Nature Conservancy of Utah, with additional assistance and cooperation from Canyonlands National Park and the Bureau of Land Management. We thank Lisa Thomas and Dusty Perkins of the NPS for their interest and support of this effort. We thank Steve Cinnamon formerly of the NPS, Billy Cardasco of Babbit Ranches, Dr. Christoper McGlone of the Ecological Restoration Institute, Dr. Matthew Loeser of Yakima Valley Community College, and Kirsten Ironside, Monica McTeague, Dr. Kathryn Thomas of the U.S. Geological Survey, and Mar-Elise Hill of Western Arizona College for devoting valuable time to expert opinion questionnaires. We especially thank Dana Witwicki, Jim DeCoster, Shane Green, and Brian Jacobs for making data available for analysis. Drs. Chris Lauver, Brandon Bestelmeyer, David Pyke, Jeff Herrick, Jayne Belnap, and Craig D. Allen contributed original ideas and feedback on this project. We thank Dana Witwicki and Jim DeCoster for constructive comments that improved this report.

References Cited

Allen-Diaz, B., and Bartolome, J.W., 1998, Sagebrush-grass vegetation dynamics: comparing classical and state-and-transition models: Ecological Applications, v. 8, p. 795–804.

Allen, C.D., 2004, Ecological patterns and environmental change in the Bandelier landscape, *in*, Kohler, T.A., ed., Archaeology of Bandelier National Monument: Village formation on the Pajarito Plateau: Albuquerque, New Mexico,University of New Mexico Press, p. 19–67.

Allen, C.D., Savage, M., Falk, D.A., Suckling, K.F., Schulke, T., Swetnam, T.W., Stacey, P.B., Morgan, P., Hoffman, M., and Klingel, J.T., 2002, Ecological restoration of southwestern ponderosa pine ecosystems—A broad perspective: Ecological Applications, v. 12, p. 1418–1433.

Allen, C.D., Macalady, A.K., Chenchouni, H., Bachelet, D., McDowell, N., Vennetier, M., Kitzberger, T., Rigling, A., Breshears, D.D., Hog, E.H., Gonzalez, P., Fensham, R., Zhang, Z., Castro, J., Demidova, N., Lim, J.L., Allard, G., Running, S.W., Semerci, A., and Cobb, N., 2010, A global overview of drought and heat-induced tree mortality reveals emerging climate change risks for forests: Forest Ecology and Management, v. 259, p. 6606–6684.

Baskin, C.C., and Baskin, J.M. 1998, Seeds: ecology, biogeography, and evolution of dormancy and germination. San Diego, California, Academic Press, 666p.

Beisner, B.E., Haydon, D.T., and Cuddington, K., 2003, Alternative stable states in ecology: Frontiers in Ecology and the Environment, v. 1, p. 376–382.

Belnap, J., 1995, Surface disturbances—their role in accelerating desertification: Environmental Monitoring Assessment, v. 37, p. 39–57.

Belnap, J., 2003, The world at your feet: desert biological soil crusts: Frontiers in Ecology Environment, v. 1, p. 181–189.

Belnap, J., and Eldridge, D.J., 2003, Disturbance and recovery of biological soil crusts, *in*, Belnap, J., and Lange, O.L., eds., Biological soil crusts—Structure, function, and management (2d ed.): Berlin, Springer-Verlag, p. 363–383.

Belnap, J., Prasse, R., and Harper, K.T., 2003, Influence of biological soil crusts on soil environments and vascular plants, *in*, Belnap, J., and Lange, O.L., eds., Biological soil crusts—Structure, function, and management (2d ed.): Berlin, Springer-Verlag, p. 281–300.

Belnap, J., Reynolds, R.L., Reheis, M.C., Phillips, S.L., Urban, F.E., and Goldstein, H.L., 2009, Sediment losses and gains across a gradient of livestock grazing and plant invasion in a cool, semi-arid grassland, Colorado Plateau, USA: Aeolian Research, v. 1, p. 27–43.

Bennetts, R.E., Gross, J.E., Cahill, K., McIntyre, C., Bingham, B., Hubbard, A., Cameron, L., Carter, S.L., 2007, Linking monitoring to management and planning—assessment points as a generalized approach: George Wright Forum, v. 24, p. 59–77.

Bestelmeyer, B.T., 2006, Threshold concepts and their use in rangeland management and restoration—The good, the bad, and the insidious: Restoration Ecology, v. 14, p. 325–329.

Bestelmeyer, B.T., Brown, J.R., Havstad, K.M., Chavez, G., Alexander, R., and Herrick, J.E., 2003, Development and use of state-and-transition models for rangelands: Journal of Range Management, v. 56, p. 114–126.

Bestelmeyer, B.T., Tugel, A.J., Peacock, G.L., Robinett, D.G., Shaver, P.L., Brown, J.R., Herrick, J.E., Sanchez, H., and Havstad, K.M., 2009, State-and-transition models for heterogeneous landscapes—A strategy for development and application: Range Ecology Management, v. 62, p. 1–15.

Bowker, M.A., and Belnap, J., 2008, A simple classification of soil types as habitats of biological soil crusts on the Colorado Plateau, USA: Journal of Vegetation Science, v. 19, p. 831–840.

Bowker, M.A., Belnap, J., Chaudhary, V.B., and Johnson, N.C., 2008, Revisiting classic water erosion models in drylands—The strong impact of biological soil crusts: Soil Biology and Biochemistry, v. 40, p. 2309–2316.

Bowker, M.A., and Belnap, J., 2007, Spatial modeling of biological soil crusts to support land management decisions: indicators of range health and conservation–restoration value based upon the potential distribution of biological soil crusts in Montezuma Castle, Tuzigoot, Walnut Canyon, and Wupatki National Monuments, Arizona: Flagstaff, Arizona, Northern Arizona University, Unpublished Report, 42 p.

Bowker, M.A., Miller, M.E., and Belote, T., 2012a, Assessment of rangeland ecosystem conditions, Salt Creek watershed and Dugout Ranch, Southeast Utah: U.S. Geological Survey Open-File Report, 2012-1061, 81 p.

Bowker, M.A., Munoz, A.A., Martinez, T., and Lau, M.K. 2012b, Rare drought-induced mortality of juniper is enhanced by edaphic stressors and influenced by stand density: Journal of Arid Environments, v. 76, p. 9–16

Bowker, M.A., Miller, M.E, Garman, S.L, and Belote, T., in press, Applying threshold concepts to conservation management of dryland ecosystems—Case studies on the Colorado Plateau, *in*, Guntenspergen, G., ed., Application of threshold concepts in natural resource decision making: Berlin, Springer.

Breshears, D.D., Cobb, N.S., Rich, P.S., Price, K.P., Allen, C.D., Balice, R.G., Romme, W.H., Kastens, J.H., Floyd, M.L., Belnap, J., Anderson, J.J., Myers, O.B., and Meyer, C.W., 2005, Regional vegetation die-off in response to global-change-type drought: Proceedings of the National Academy of Sciences, v. 102, p.15144–15148

Briske, D.D., Fuhlendorf, S.D., and Smeins, F.E., 2006, A unified framework for assessment and application of ecological thresholds: Rangeland Ecology and Management, v. 59, p.225–236.

Briske, D.D., Bestelmeyer, B.T., Stringham, T.K., and Shaver, P.L., 2008, Recommendations for development of resilience-based state-and-transition models: Rangeland Ecology and Management, v. 61, p. 359–367.

Brockway, D.G., Gatewood, R.G., and Paris, R.B., 2002. Restoring grassland savannas from degraded pinyon-juniper woodlands—Effects of mechanical overstory reduction and slash treatment alternatives: Journal of Environmental Management, v. 64, p.179–197.

Chapin III, F.S., Torn, M.S., and Tateno, M., 1996, Principles of ecosystem sustainability: American Naturalist, v. 148, p. 1016–1037.

Chaudhary, V.B., Bowker, M.A., O'Dell, T.E., Grace, J.B., Redman, A.E., Johnson, N.C., and Rillig, M., 2009, Untangling the biological controls on soil stability in semi-arid shrublands: Ecological Applications, v. 40, p. 2309–2316.

Cinnamon, S.K., 1988, The vegetation community of Cedar Canyon, Wupatki National Monument as influenced by prehistoric and historic environmental change: Flagstaff, Arizona, Northern Arizona University, Master of Science thesis, 98 p.

Clark, D., Dela Cruz, M., Clark, T., Coles, J., Topp, S., Evenden, A., Wight, A., Wakefield, G., Von Loh, J., 2009, Vegetation classification and mapping project report, Capitol Reef National Park: Fort Collins, Colorado, National Park Service Natural Resource Technical Report NPS/NCPN/NRTR–2009/187, 882 p.

Coles, J., Tendick, A., Manis, G., Wight, A., Wakefield, G., Von Loh, J., and Evenden, A., 2009, Vegetation classification and mapping project report, Arches National Park: Fort Collins, Colorado, National Park Service Natural Resource Technical Report NPS/NCPN/NRTR–2009/253, 544 p.

Cook, C.N., Hockings, M., and Carter, R.W., 2010, Conservation in the dark? The information used to support management decisions: Frontiers in Ecology and the Environment, v. 8, p. 181–186.

Davenport, D.W., Breshears, D.D., Wilcox, B.P., and Allen, C.D., 1998, Viewpoint—Sustainability of pinyon-juniper ecosystems, a unifying perspective of soil erosion thresholds: Journal of Range Management, v. 51, p. 231–240.

Davidson, D.W., Bowker, M.A., George, D., Phillips, S.L., and Belnap, J., 2002, Treatment effects on performance of N-fixing lichens in disturbed soil crusts on the Colorado Plateau: Ecological Applications, v. 12, p. 1391–1405.

De'ath, G., and Fabricius, K.E., 2000, Classification and regression trees; a powerful yet simple technique for ecological data analysis: Ecology, v. 81, p. 3178–3192.

DeCoster, J.K., and Swan, M.C., 2009a, Integrated upland vegetation and soils monitoring for Wupatki National Monument—2008 summary report: Fort Collins, Colorado, National Park Service Natural Resource Data Series NPS/SCPN/NRDS–2009/022, 22 p.

DeCoster, J.K., and Swan, M.C., 2009b, Integrated upland vegetation and soils monitoring for Petrified Forest National Park—2007 summary report: Fort Collins, Colorado, National Park Service Natural Resource Data Series NPS/ SCPN/NRDS–2009/005, 23 p.

DeCoster, J.K., and Swan, MC., 2011, Integrated upland vegetation and soils monitoring for Bandelier National Monument—2009 summary report: Fort Collins, Colorado, National Park Service Natural Resource Data Series NPS/SCPN/NRDS–2011/168, 25 p.

Digiovinazzo, P., Ficetola, G.F., Bottoni, L., Andreis, C., and Padoa-Schioppa, E., 2010, Ecological thresholds in herb communities for the management of suburban fragmented forests: Forest Ecology and Management, v. 259, p. 343–349.

Doughty, J.W., 1971, Soil survey and range site and condition inventory. Wupatki National Monuments, Arizona. A special report. Portland, Oregon, U.S. Department of Agriculture, Soil Conservation Service, 39 p.

Dufrene, M., and Legendre, P., 1997, Species assemblages and indicator species—The need for a flexible asymmetrical approach: Ecological Monographs, v. 67, p. 345-366.

Equihua, M., 1990, Fuzzy clustering of ecological data: Journal of Ecology, v. 78, p.519.

Escudero, A., Martinez, I., de la Cruz, A., Otalora, M.A.G., and Maestre, F.T., 2007, Soil lichens have species-specific effects on the seedling emergence of three gypsophile plant species: Journal of Arid Environments, v. 70, p. 18–28.

Evans, R.D., and Lange, O.L., 2003, Biological soil crusts and ecosystem nitrogen and carbon dynamics, *in*, Belnap, J., and Lange, O.L., eds., Biological soil crusts—Structure, function, and management (2d ed.): Berlin, Springer-Verlag, p. 263–280.

Fancy, S.G., Gross, J.E., and Carter, S.L., 2009, Monitoring the condition of natural resources in U.S. National Parks: Environmental Monitoring and Assessment, v. 151, p. 161–174.

Ficetola, G.F., and Denoël, M., 2009, Ecological thresholds: an assessment of methods to identify abrupt changes in species-habitat relationships: Ecography, v. 32, p. 1075–1084.

Field, S.A., Tyre, A.J., Jonzén, N., Rhodes, J.R., and Possingham, H.P., 2004, Minimizing the cost of environmental management decision by optimizing statistical thresholds: Ecology Letters, v. 7, p. 669–675.

Friedel, M.H., 1991, Range condition assessment and the concept of thresholds—A viewpoint: Journal of Range Management, v. 44, p. 422-426.

Ford, P.L., 1999, Response of buffalograss (*Buchloe dactyloides*) and blue grama (*Bouteloua gracilis*) to fire: Great Plains Research, v. 9, p. 261–76.

Gitlin, A.R., Sthultz, C.M., Bowker, M.A., Stumpf, S., Paxton, K.L., Kennedy, K., Munoz, A., Bailey, J.K., and Whitham, T.G., 2006, Mortality gradients within and among dominant plant populations as barometers of ecosystem change during extreme drought: Conservation Biology, v. 20, p. 1477–1486.

Groffman, P., Baron, J., Blett, T., Gold, A., Goodman, I., Gunderson, L., Levinson, B., Palmer, M., Paerl, H., Peterson, G., Poff, N., Rejeski, D., Reynolds, J., Turner, M., Weathers, K., and Wiens, J., 2006, Ecological thresholds—The key to successful environmental management or an important concept with no practical application?: Ecosystems, v. 9, p. 1–13.

Hansen, M., Coles, J., Thomas, K.A., Cogan, K., Reid, M., Von Loh, J., and Schulz, K., 2004, USGS-NPS national vegetation mapping program—Wupatki National Monument, Arizona, vegetation classification and distribution: Flagstaff, Arizona, Southwest Biological Science Center, U.S Geological Survey, 229 p.

Hassler, F, 2006, Dynamics of juniper invaded grasslands and old growth woodlands at Wupatki National Monument, Northern Arizona, USA: Flagstaff, Arizona, Northern Arizona University, Master of Science thesis, 121 p.

Hastings, B.F., Smith, F.M., and Jacobs, B.F., 2003, Rapidly eroding pinon-juniper woodlands in New Mexico—Response to slash treatment: Journal of Environmental Quality, v. 32, p. 1290–1298.

Herrick, J.E., 2000, Soil quality: an indicator of sustainable management?: Applied Soil Ecology, v. 15, p. 75–84.

Herrick, J.E., Whitford, W.G., and Walton, M., 2001, Field soil aggregate stability kit for soil quality and rangeland health evaluations: Catena, v. 44, p. 27–35.

Herrick, J.E., Van Zee, J.W., Havstad, K.M., Burkett, L.M., and Whitford, W.G., 2005, Monitoring manual for grassland, shrubland and savanna ecosystems. Volume I—Quick start: Las Cruces, New Mexico, USDA-ARS Jornada Experimental Range, 199 p.

Hibner, C.D., 2000, Special project soil survey of Bandelier National Monument—U.S. Department of Agriculture, interim report: Santa Fe, New Mexico, Natural Resources Conservation Service, 346 p.

Hintze, J., 2004, NCSS, Number Cruncher Statistical Systems (software): Kaysville, Utah.

Hobbs, R.J., and Norton, D.A., 1996, Towards a conceptual framework for restoration ecology: Restoration Ecology, v. 4, p. 93–110.

Hodgkinson, H.S., 1987, Relationship of saltbush species to soil chemical properties: Journal of Range Management, v. 40, p. 23–26.

Ironside, K., 2006, Climate change research in national parks—Paleoecology, policy, and modeling the future: Flagstaff, Arizona, Northern Arizona University, Master of Science thesis, 206 p.

Jacobs, B.F., 2002, Reintroduction of fire maintains structure of mechanically restored Pinyon-Juniper Savannah (New Mexico): Ecological Restoration, v. 20, p. 207–208.

Jacobs, B.F., Gatewood, R.G., and Allen, C.D., 2002, Watershed restoration in degraded pinon-juniper woodlands—A paire watershed study 1996-1998(9): Los Alamos, New Mexico, Bandelier National Park, 67 p.

Jacques, C.N., Sievers, J.D., Jenks, J.A., Sexton, C.L., and Roddy, D.E., 2006, Evaluating diet composition of pronghorn in Wind Cave National ParK, South Dakota: Prairie Naturalist, v. 38, p. 239–250.

Jameson, D.A., 1962, Effects of burning on a Galleta-Black Grama Range invaded by juniper: Ecology, v. 43, p. 760–763.

King, E.G., and Hobbs, R.J., 2006, Identifying linkages among conceptual models of ecosystem degradation and restoration—Towards an integrative framework: Restoration Ecology, v. 14, p. 369–378.

Kleiner, E.F., and Harper, K.T. 1972, Environment and community organization in grasslands of Canyonlands National Park: Ecology, v. 53, p. 299–309.

Ladenburger, C.G.,Hilda, A.L., Kazmerb, D.J., and Munn, L.C., 2006, Soil salinity patterns in *Tamarix* invasions in the Bighorn Basin, Wyoming, USA: Journal of Arid Environments, v. 65, p. 111–128.

Linstone, H.A., Turoff, M.A., eds., 1975, The Delphi method—Techniques and applications: Reading, Massachussets, Addison-Wesley, 615 p.

May, R.M., 1973, Stability and complexity in model ecosystems: Princeton, New Jersey, Princeton University Press, 292 p.

McCune, B.P., and Grace, J.B., 2002, Analysis of ecological communities: Gleneden Beach, Oregon, MJM Software Design, 284 p.

Miller, M.E., Witwicki, D.L., Mann, R.K., and Tancreto, N.J., 2007, Field evaluation of sampling methods for long-term monitoring of upland ecosystems on the Colorado Plateau: U.S. Geological Survey Open File Report 2007–1243, 196 p.

Miller, M.E., 2008, Broad-scale assessment of rangeland health, Grand Staircase-Escalante National Monument, USA: Rangeland Ecology and Management, v. 63, p. 249–262.

Miller, M.E., Belote, R.T., Bowker, M.A., and Garman, S.L., 2011, Alternative states of a semiarid grassland ecosystem—Implications for ecosystem services: Ecosphere, v. 2 (5), p. 1-18.

Miller, M.L., 1975, Soil survey of Apache County, Arizona, central part: Washington, D.C., U.S. Department of Agriculture, Soil Conservation Service, 71 p.

Miller, R.F., and Wigand, P.E., 1994, Holocene changes in semi-arid pinyon-juniper woodlands: BioScience, v. 44, p. 465–474.

Muradian, R., 2001, Ecological thresholds—A survey: Ecological Economics, v. 38, p. 7–24.

Natural Resources Conservation Service,, 1991, Soil survey of Canyonlands area, Utah, parts of Grand and San Juan Counties: Washington, D.C., US Department of Agriculture, Natural Resource Conservation Service, 57 p.

Natural Resources Conservation Service, 2010, The PLANTS database (*http://plants.usda.gov*, 21 July 2010): The U.S. Department of Agriculture PLANTS Web Site, accessed July 21, 2010, at *http://plants.usda.gov/*

National Park Service, 2002, Final environmental impact statement general management plan. Wupatki National Monument, Arizona: Flagstaff, Arizona, U.S. Department of the Interior, National Park Service, 333 p.

National Park Service, 2005, Fire Management Plan Environmental Assessment/Assessment of effect. Flagstaff, Arizona, Flagstaff Area National Monuments, National Park Service, 187 p.

Neff, J.C., Reynolds, R.L., Belnap, J., and Lamothe, P., 2005, Multi-decadal impacts of grazing on soil physical and biogeochemical properties in southeast Utah: Ecological Applications, v. 15, p. 87–95.

Nichols, J.D., and Williams, B.K., 2006, Monitoring for conservation: Trends in Ecology and Evolution, v. 21, p. 668–673.

O'Dell, T., Garman, S., Evenden, A., Beer, M., Nance, E., Perry, D., DenBleyker, R., Sharrow, D., Wynn, K., Brown, J., Miller, M., and Thomas, L., 2005, Northern Colorado Plateau inventory and monitoring network, vital signs monitoring plan: Moab, Utah, National Park Service, 175 p.

Oliver, I., 2002, Introduction to an expert panel based approach for assessment of vegetation condition within the context of biodiversity conservation: Ecological Management and Restoration, v. 3, p. 227–229.

Paine, R.T., Tegner, M.J., and Johnson, E.A., 1998, Compounded perturbations yield ecological surprises: Ecosystems, v. 1, p. 535–545.

Parker, C.L., 2009, Evaluating juniper cover change form 1936–1997 in the Wupatki Area using repeat aerial photography: Flagstaff, Arizona, Northern Arizona University, Master of Science thesis, 178 p.

Peters, D.C., Pielke Sr., R.A., Bestelmeyer, B.T., Allen, C.D., Munson-McGee, S., and Havstad, K.M., 2004, Cross-scale interactions, nonlinearities, and forecasting catastrophic events: Proceedings of the National Academy of Sciences, v. 101, p. 15130–15135.

Pyke, D.A., Herrick, J.E., Shaver, P., and Pellant, M., 2002, Rangeland health attributes and indicators for qualitative assessment: Journal of Range Management, v. 55, p. 584-597.

Rapport, D.J., and Whitford, W.G., 1999, How ecosystems respond to stress—Common properties of arid and aquatic systems: BioScience, v. 49, p. 193–203.

Reynolds, R.L., Belnap, J., Reheis, M.C., Lamothe, P., and Luiszer, F., 2001, Aeolian dust in Colorado Plateau soils—Nutrient inputs and recent change in source: Proceedings of the National Academy of Sciences, v. 98, p. 7123–7127.

Scheffer, M., Hosper, S.H., Meijer, M.L., and Moss, B., 1993, Alternative equilibria in shallow lakes: Trends in Ecology and Evolution, v. 8, p. 275–279.

Scheffer, M., Carpenter, S., Foley, J.A., Folke, C., and Walker, B., 2001, Catastrophic shifts in ecosystems: Nature, v. 413, p. 591–596.

Scott, M.L., Brasher, A.M.D., Reynolds, E., Caires, A., and Miller, M.E., 2005, The structure and functioning of riparian and aquatic ecosystems of the Colorado Plateau—Conceptual models to inform long-term ecological monitoring: U.S. Geological Survey, Fort Collins, Colorado, 115 p.

Shaw, J.R., and Cooper, T.J., 2008, Linkages among watersheds, stream reaches,and riparian vegetation in dryland ephemeral stream networks: Journal of Hydrology, v. 350, p. 68–82.

Soil Conservation Service, 1983, Soil survey of Coconino County area, Arizona, central part: Washington, D.C., U.S. Department of Agriculture, Soil Conservation Service, 212 p.

Soulé, M.E., 1985, What is conservation biology?: Bioscience, v. 35, p. 727–734.

Stringham, T.K., Krueger, W.C., and Thomas, D.R., 2001, Application of non-equilibrium ecology to rangeland riparian zones: Journal of Range Management, v. 54, p. 210–217.

Suding, K.N., Gross, K.L., and Houseman, G.R., 2004, Alternative states and positive feedbacks in restoration ecology: Trends in Ecology and Evolution, v. 19, p. 46–53.

Suding, K.N., and Hobbs, R.J., 2009, Threshold models in restoration and conservation—A new framework: Trends in Ecology and Evolution, v. 24, p. 271–279.

Thomas, L.P., Hendrie, M.N., Lauver, C.L., Monroe, S.A., Tancreto, N.J., Garman, S.L., and Miller, M.E., 2006, Vital signs monitoring plan for the southern Colorado Plateau network, natural resource report: Flagstaff, Arizona: National Park Service NPS/SCPN/NRR-2006/002, 128 p.

Thomas, K.A., Hansen, M., and Seger, C., 2003, Part 1—Vegetation of Petrified Forest National Park, Arizona: Flagstaff, Arizona, Southwest Biological Science Center, US Geological Survey, 125 p.

Thomas, K.A., McTeague, M.L., Cully, A., Schulz, K., and Hutchinson, J.M.S. 2009, Vegetation classification and distribution mapping report—Petrified Forest National Park: Fort Collins, Colorado, National Park Service National Resource Technical Report NPS/SCPN/NRTR—2009/273, 294 p.

Toms, J.D., and Lesperance, M.L., 2003, Piecewise regression—A tool for identifying ecological thresholds: Ecology, v. 84, p. 2034–2041.

Ungar, I.A., 1966, Salt tolerance of plants growing in saline areas of Kansas and Oklahoma: Ecology, v. 47, p. 154–155.

Warren, S.D., 2003, Synopsis—Influence of biological soil crusts on arid land hydrology and soil stability, *in*, Belnap, J., and Lange, O.L., eds., Biological soil crusts—Structure, function, and management (2d ed.): Berlin, Springer-Verlag, p. 349–360.

Walker, B., and Meyers, J.A., 2004, Thresholds in ecological and social-ecological systems—A developing database: Ecology and Society, v. 9, p. 3.

Whisenant, S.G., 1999, Repairing damaged wildlands—A process-oriented, landscape-scale approach: Cambridge University Press, Cambridge, United Kingdom, 328 p.

Witwicki, D., 2009a, Integrated upland monitoring in Canyonlands National Park—Annual report 2008: Fort Collins, Colorado, National Park Service Natural Resource Technical Report NPS/NCPN/NRTR - 2009/236, 36 p.

Witwicki D. 2009b. Integrated upland monitoring in Capitol Reef National Park—Annual report 2008. Fort Collins, Colorado: National Park Service Natural Resource Technical Report NPS/NCPN/NRTR - 2009/237, 38 p.

Appendix A. Expert Opinion Surveys

We constructed email-based questionnaires in two phases: (1) model calibration, and (2) estimation of tipping and assessment points in indicators that enable detection of proximity to threshold crossings. This appendix documents the expert opinion surveys used in the Limy uplands case study. We identified a list of potential expert consultants from the authors of relevant literature, and from professional interactions. We initially contacted selected experts by email to gauge interest. Of eight people contacted, five were willing to participate. We received four phase 1 surveys with an average response time of 9 days (we had requested return within 7 days). We revised the model, according to respondent comments and calculated an aggregate confidence value. The second phase of the survey was more focused on thresholds associated with a key transition (from reference grasslands to savannized ecosystems, see). We emailed the phase 2 surveys to the four respondents who had previously returned phase 1 surveys, in addition to one new respondent and several previous candidates who had not been able to respond. We received six with an average response time of 20 days. Survey format is documented below (*** = required question).

Phase 1 Survey: ***1) Please identify any states or phases which should be omitted from the state-and-transition model. You may select more than one.

2) Please identify any manageable states or phases which are currently not in the model, but should be added to the state and transition model.
[Please briefly list structural properties, like dominant species or overall vegetative cover (whatever you feel is important to mention), and functional properties and processes such as fire return intervals or low soil stability. When you list properties please think about and indicate if they are dynamic or inherent and if they contribute to the resistance or resilience of the state or phase. Please indicate any feedback mechanisms which tend to maintain these states. If you are identifying a phase, is it at-risk? Let us know about appropriate literature if you know of it.]

***3) Please identify any transitions which should be omitted from the state-and-transition model. You may select more than one.

4) Please identify any transitions which are currently not in the model but should be added to the state-and-transition model.
[For each addition, provide the starting state and ending state for which the transition applies. Identify plausible trigger mechanisms. Additionally, please provide a brief explanation of the process that brings about the transition, for example, fire, insect outbreak, drought, or grazing. Please note the dominant scale of the trigger mechanism and the importance of temporal convergence and order with other mechanisms (for example simultaneous drought and grazing may function as a trigger when either alone do not). Additionally suggest monitorable indicators.]

***5) Please estimate your overall confidence that a new revised model which takes into account your proposed modifications is the correct model of the most important ecosystem states, processes, and dynamics of the ecosite in question.
[Please answer on a subjective scale of 0–100 percent certainty. Enter any value in this range. To help your answer: 0 percent means, "It's anyone's guess, this model is no better than any other model"; 50 percent means, "Because this model is reasonable, I would tend to believe it until evidence to the

contrary is presented"; 100 precent means, "The model is so well-supported by evidence and accumulated knowledge, that I am certain it is correct."]

6) If your level of confidence in any particular state or transition differs from the value above please estimate your confidence for that model component in the appropriate box. In case you are estimating a confidence in a state or transition suggested by you in questions 2 and 4, please use the "other" options to identify it.
[If you do not provide answers to question 6 we will assume they are the same as the answers to

question 5 in all cases.]

***7) Please take a moment to think of any scientist or other person who is, to your knowledge, the best qualified to develop a state-and-transition model for this ecosite. This person could be yourself or any other person. "Best" qualified may or may not mean highly qualified; sometimes no one is highly qualified. In the hypothetical scenario that this person had prepared a state-and-transition model for this ecosite using all of the data, knowledge, and experience available to them, estimate how much confidence you would have that it is the correct model of the most important ecosystem states, processes, and dynamics of the ecosite in question.
[Please answer on a subjective scale of 0–100 percent certainty]

8.) Who is the best qualified person (from question 7) to develop this state-and-transition model? This response will help us ensure we have contacted all of the right people.

Phase 2 Survey: ***1) Please estimate your overall confidence that this model, which takes into account proposed modifications from previous surveys, is the correct model of the most important ecosystem states, processes, and dynamics of the ecosite in question.
[Please answer on a subjective scale of 0–100 percent certainty]

2) If your level of confidence in any particular state or transition differs from the value above, please identify and estimate your confidence for that model component in the appropriate box.
[example answer: S1P2, 75 percent; T4, 55 percent; T13, 30 percent]

***3) Please take a moment to think of any scientist or other person who is, to your knowledge, the best qualified to develop a state-and-transition model for this ecosite. This person could be yourself, or any other person. "Best" qualified may or may not mean highly qualified; sometimes no one is highly qualified. In the hypothetical scenario that this person had prepared a state-and-transition model for this ecosite using all of the data, knowledge, and experience available to them, estimate how much confidence you would have that it is the correct model of the most important ecosystem states, processes, and dynamics of the ecosite in question.
[Please answer on a subjective scale of 0–100 percent certainty]

For transition 8 (T8), we will present you with several relevant indicators in a spreadsheet response matrix and prompt you to answer 6 questions, filling in your answers in the matrix. To keep the model broad, the indicators apply to the whole Limy uplands ecological site, inside and outside of Wupatki, and encompassing different grazing and fire suppression regimes:

Stocking rate: An allotment- or pasture-scale measure of grazing pressure which may or may not account for seasonality (may poorly reflect more localized stock use, for example near water). May trigger T8 if high enough.
Density of cowpies: A site-scale measure of grazing pressure. May trigger T8 if high enough.
Density of pronghorn (A. americana) pellet groups: A site-scale measure of native browser activity. May reverse T8 as long as T8 has not progressed beyond restoration threshold.
Time since fire: A site-scale measure of either grazing-triggered reduction of fuels or fire suppression practices. May trigger T8 if high enough.
Total plant cover: An easy to measure surrogate for biomass and index of fuel load. Decreases as T8 progresses.
Basal plant cover plus litter: An index related both to amount and connectivity of fuel. Decreases as T8 progresses.
Average length of bare patches: An inverse measure of fuel connectivity. A bare patch is devoid of plant basal cover or litter. Increases as T8 progresses.
Average length of combustible patches: A measure of connectivity. Decreases as T8 progresses.
Number of trees per hectare: A measure of colonization rates and a glimpse of the future if trees mature. Increases as T8 progresses.
Average tree height: A measure of tree resistance to fire. Increases as T8 progresses, may signal completion of transition.

For each indicator we will ask you to estimate the preventative threshold point and the restoration threshold point in the specified units (except for three indicators where we feel only preventative thresholds apply). Answer based on past experience, accumulated knowledge, and general principles. We do not expect anyone to know the answer— we are just collecting opinions and educated guesses as a means of estimating a plausible range of threshold values. If you wish, you may consult a data source that you are already aware of, but we do not expect you to undertake an extensive literature review to find new information. As a reference, to help you get within the ballpark, we have provided estimates of current status of monitoring plots, or other useful reference points, when available. You may interpret "current status" as belonging to whichever state or phase you think is correct. Do not be worried if you do not have much confidence in your estimate, you also will be asked to rate your confidence in your estimate, and your confidence in anyone's estimate. Confidence will be taken into account and will be a part of the final product. Just to reiterate, we are interested in your low confidence estimates, too.

For questions 4 and 5, we would like you to try and complete at least 50 percent of yellow portion of the response table, even if your confidence in your answers is low. The more complete it is, the better. If you truly have no idea whatsoever about the answer to a particular question (about 0 percent confidence), you may leave it blank, but please try if you can.

***4) Please estimate the **preventative** threshold, the last point during a transition at which the possibility of reversal using passive restoration still exists. Please answer in appropriate units in response matrix below.

***5) Please estimate the **restoration** threshold, the point at which transition has occurred or is imminent, even if passive restoration is undertaken. Beyond this point, active restoration is required to reverse a transition. Please answer in appropriate units in response matrix below.

6) Would you add any indicators to this list that would be crucial in tracking transition 8? If so please type in the indicator (in the "other indicator" cells) and units in appropriate boxes in the response matrix below, and provide your corresponding preventative and restoration threshold estimates there.

***7) Overall, please estimate your confidence in your threshold estimates, including any provided in question 4.
[Please answer on a subjective scale of 0–100 percent certainty.]

***8) Please take a moment to think of any scientist or other person who is, to your knowledge, the best qualified to estimate the values you estimated in questions 1 and 2. This person could be yourself, or any other person. "Best" qualified may or may not mean highly qualified; sometimes no one is highly qualified. In the hypothetical scenario that this person had made these estimates, using all of the data, knowledge, and experience available to them, estimate how much confidence you would have that they are the correct values.
[use the same scale as question 3, 0–100 percent]

9) Now please consider, for any *individual* threshold estimates you provided, if any of the values of "confidence in your own estimate" or "confidence in anyone's estimates" differ from the answers to questions 7 and 8. If so, fill them into the response matrix below.

Appendix B. Assessment and Tipping Points Quick Reference

[Summary of all assessment and tipping point estimates discussed in this report. In general, we refer to a transition probability of 95 percent as a tipping point and provide assessment points corresponding to 5 percent, 25 percent, and 50 percent transition probabilities. a = Transition is extremely abrupt between 26–27 percent exotic plant cover. b = Maximal transition probability less than 95 percent. c = Multiple assessment and tipping points are possible, refer to figure 9. d = Based on pooled blackbrush shrublands and wooded shrublands from semidesert shallow sandy loam and desert shallow sandy loam. Equation addresses degree of degradation of soil aggregate stability rather than transition probability. A 95 percent reduction in soil aggregate stability is not plausible in our model. e = Expert opinion surveys did not distinguish among different transition probabilities, rather a single assessment point was requested]

Ecological Site	Transition	Indicator	"Assessment point 1" (transition prob. 5%)	"Assessment point 2" (transition prob. 25%)	"Assessment point 3" (transition prob. 50%)	"Tipping point" (transition prob. 95%)
Semidesert sandy loam (Fourwing saltbush)	T6: Biological crust dominated-invaded	Soil aggregate stability	5.2	5.0	4.9	4.7
	to Invaded grassland	Magnetic susceptibility	0.20	0.16	0.14	0.10
		Surface roughness	14.8	10.5	8.8	5.4
		Biocrust cover (%)	49	30	22.5	7.5
	T9: Invaded grassland to Annualized	Relative exotic cover (%)	a	a	a	26%
Mesa top pinyon-juniper	T6: Productive woodlands	Proportional forb cover	0.34	0.23	0.16	b
	to Open woodlands	Proportional *P. edulis* cover	0.005	0.007	0.009	b
	T7: Unproductive woodlands	Proportional litter cover	0.33	0.43	0.49	0.6
	to Open woodlands	Proportional bare ground cover	0.36	0.31	0.28	0.23
	T9: Open woodlands	Proportional herbaceous cover	c	c	c	c
	to Restored savannas	Proportional litter cover	c	c	c	c
Semidesert shallow sandy loam (Utah juniper & pinyon pine)	T1: Wooded shrublands-biocrusted to wooded shrublands	Biocrust cover (%)	38.9[d]	28.3[d]	15.1[d]	d

Ecological site	State transition	Variable				
	T3: Blackbruhs shrublands-biocrusted to blackbrush shrublands	Biocrust cover (%)	38.9[d]	28.3[d]	15.1[d]	d
	T9: Grassy shrublands to Subshrub dominated-invaded	Biocrust cover (%)		1.44	1.32	
		Total plant cover (%)		26.92	20.89	
		Exotic annual relative cover (%)		0.25	0.54	
Semidesert shallow sandy loam (Utah juniper & pinyon pine)	T1: Blackbruhs shrublands-biocrusted to blackbrush shrublands	Biocrust cover (%)	38.9[d]	28.3[d]	15.1[d]	d
Semidesert stony loam (Shadscale)	T1: Palatable shrublands to Less-palatable shrublands	decreasers:increasers	0.51	0.3	0.18	b
	T3: Less-palatable shrublands to Grazing-impacted shrublands	grasses:shrubs	0.41	0.47	0.51	0.6
	T5: Grazing-impacted shrublands to Annualized	Proportional exotic cover	0.271	0.275	0.277	0.279
Clayey fans	T6: Less-palatable shrublands to Annualized	Total plant cover (%)	29.0	20.0	14.5	0
Limy uplands	T8: Rhizomatous grasslands to Savannized	time since fire (y)		22.4[e]		28.0
		total plant cover (%)		18.8[e]		7.7
		basal cover incl. litter (%)		17.0[e]		9.7
		interspace length (cm)		66.7[e]		-
		average tree height (m)		0.86[e]		1.62